Praise for *The One Hour Plan*

"It took me a long time to learn that, in business, less is usually more. Joe Calhoon's system for how to create a clear and compelling business plan is the best I've ever seen!"

—**Mac Anderson, Founder, Successories and Simple Truths**

"If I only had one hour per day to work on my business, I would spend it learning and implementing *The One Hour Plan*. . . . It is easier and more fun, to arrive at a destination if you visualize it beforehand."

—**Michael Drever, CEO and Founder,
Expedia CruiseShipCenters**

"It has been said that 'without vision, the people perish.' You are about to discover a life-changing approach for gaining fresh vision and a renewed sense of purpose for every aspect of your life."

—**Glenna Salsbury, CSP,
CPAE Speaker Hall of Fame,
Author of *The Art of the Fresh Start***

"Joe has distilled a complex topic into a very practical, efficient, and effective body of valuable information. The content prompts the imagination and stimulates the energy to fulfill a task that is essential for success. If it is true that 'only the disciplined are free,' then this reading will free the reader as they benefit from their investment of time."

—**Fred Pryor, Founder, Fred Pryor Seminars**

"Joe Calhoon lays out a methodology for business . . . and for life. It is amazingly simple, but powerfully effective. If you're not where you want to be—this is the book for you!"

—**Bob Dickinson, Former President and CEO,
Carnival Cruise Lines**

"Most everyone knows that they should plan, yet so many don't do it efficiently or effectively, if they do it at all. They say they don't have time to do it right, but I have long suspected the real issue is they simply don't know how. *The One Hour Plan for Growth* provides any leader interested in growth with the 'how' they need to get planning right, right now."

—**Steven Little,
Author of *The 7 Irrefutable Rules of
Small Business Growth***

"Joe Calhoon nails it. . . . [T]his is the handbook you always 'wished you had!' This powerful process starts with vision and mission, then puts the other planning elements into a condensed form that can lead any business to greater growth and success. We wish we had this book when we started our business 40 years ago."

—Naomi Rhode, CSP, CPAE Speaker Hall of Fame,
Cofounder SmartPractice

"The One Hour Plan for Growth helps crystallize your thinking . . . FAST, and gets your team on the same page with you . . . FAST!"

—Bobb Biehl,
Executive Mentor, BobbBiehl.com

"Congratulations on creating this simple, direct, and useful tool. Creating a plan and leading with a simple vision creates a positive, fun and creative work environment where an engaged team can perform beyond even their own expectations. The planning process is often daunting, time consuming, and frequently creates too complex a document that quickly becomes shelved. You have boiled the process down to a few simple bites—a business leader would be wise to spend a few hours assessing their business though this lens."

—Augie Grasis,
Founder & Chairman, Handmark, Inc.

"Joe Calhoon is an expert at making the growth planning process simple. *The One Hour Plan for Growth* reinforces an old personalized principle of 'KISS'— 'Keep it Simple Steve.' This book is a must read for every team member where leadership is committed to growth. Now there is a book which makes the growth planning process simple and practical, and shares a case study from my favorite BBQ restaurant, Jack Stack."

—Stephen Linnemann, Vice President,
Burns & McDonnell Engineering Co.

"Joe Calhoon's, *One Hour Plan for Growth* is a powerful, clear, and simplified method to make the oft incomplete job of planning complete. The magic of it for me is the single sheet of paper. Joe's excellent simplification, clarification, and brevity are the keys to getting your organization committed and focused."

—Barnett Helzberg, Founder,
Helzberg Entrepreneurial Mentoring Program

"This insightful book is both methodical and inspiring. Learn how to execute the perfect plan for professional growth and success by implementing these solid ideas."

—**Dr. Nido Qubein, President,
High Point University; Chairman, Great Harvest Bread Co.**

"Strategic planning too often is assigned to the domain of outside consultants. The process becomes long, tedious, and stale without the necessary bias for action. *The One Hour Plan for Growth* breaks through this mindset. Joe Calhoon's approach is powerfully simple and results oriented. I have benefitted from Joe's experience and clear thinking for years, and this book captures him at his best!"

—**Hans Helmerich, President and CEO,
Helmerich & Payne, Inc.**

"Every entrepreneur and leader knows the importance of a strategic plan, but remarkably, too many attempt to brave the dangerous waters of business without one. Joe Calhoon's, *The One Hour Plan for Growth* launches us from knowing to doing by removing the pain and excuses of developing and executing a high-octane strategic plan. Joe's plan helps us live the credo that Action Is Power."

—**Larry Broughton, Founder, BroughtonHotels.com;
ToolsForSuccess.com; and LarryBroughton.net**

"Joe saves you from the old saying, 'If you don't know where you're going, you'll probably end up somewhere else,' to 'When you know where you're going, you'll end up where you want to be.' And . . . he delivers that with simplicity, elegance, and a step-by-step process."

—**Ron Willingham, Founder,
LifeScript Learning**

"I've always been a great believer in Joe's simplified planning process. His *One Hour Plan for Growth* takes the concept to an entirely different level—one that will help any business develop actionable plans that get results—faster, better, and easier."

—**Bob Pike CSP, CPAE,
Chairman/CEO, The Bob Pike Group**

The ONE HOUR PLAN for GROWTH

HOW A **SINGLE SHEET OF PAPER** CAN TAKE YOUR BUSINESS TO THE **NEXT LEVEL**

JOE CALHOON

WILEY

John Wiley & Sons, Inc.

Published by John Wiley & Sons, Inc., Hoboken, New Jersey.
Published simultaneously in Canada.

For general information on our other products and services or for technical support, please contact our Customer Care Department within the United States at (800) 762-2974, outside the United States at (317) 572-3993 or fax (317) 572-4002.

Wiley also publishes its books in a variety of electronic formats. Some content that appears in print may not be available in electronic books. For more information about Wiley products, visit our web site at www.wiley.com.

Library of Congress Cataloging-in-Publication Data:

Calhoon, Joe, 1952–
The one hour plan for growth : how a single sheet of paper can take your business to the next level / Joe Calhoon.
p. cm.
Includes index.
ISBN 978-0-470-88096-8 (pbk.); 978-0-470-90637-8 (ebk);
978-0-470-90638-5 (ebk); 978-0-470-90639-2 (ebk)
1. Business planning. 2. Strategic planning. I. Title.
HD30.28.C343 2011
658.4'012–dc22   2010018649

Printed in the United States of America

10 9 8 7 6 5 4 3 2 1

Contents

Foreword   *Stephen R. Covey*   *ix*

Acknowledgments   *xiii*

Introduction: Are You Ready to Get Started?   *xv*

PART I   **PLANNING FOR GROWTH**   **1**

Chapter 1   The Shortcut   3

Chapter 2   An Overview of the One Hour Plan   5

PART II   **WHERE DO YOU WANT TO GO?**   **21**

Chapter 3   **Vision:** What Big Goal Will Inspire You
                and Your Team? (6 minutes)   23

Chapter 4   **The Customer-Centered Mission Statement:**
                What Contribution Do You Make to
                Your Customers' Lives? (6 minutes)   35

Chapter 5   **Values:** What Standards Will Help Your
                Team Enjoy Working Together? (6 minutes)   47

Chapter 6   **Objectives:** How Will You Measure
                Success? (7 minutes)   69

PART III **WHERE ARE YOU NOW?** **83**

Chapter 7 Facing the Brutal Realities: What Are the
Big Issues that Must Be Addressed? (10 minutes) 85

PART IV **HOW WILL YOU GET FROM HERE TO THERE?** **95**

Chapter 8 Strategies: What Are the Major Categories of
Work to Be Done? (15 minutes) 97

Chapter 9 Priorities: Who Will Do What by
When? (10 minutes) 141

Chapter 10 Action Plans: Putting It on the Calendar
and Getting It Done 155

PART V **ENGAGING YOUR TEAM** **161**

Chapter 11 What's Next?: How to Create and Execute a
Team Plan for Years to Come 163

Appendix 1—Organizational Health Assessment 173

Appendix 2—How to Conduct a SWOT Analysis 185

About the Author 191

Additional Planning Resources 193

Foreword

Stephen R. Covey

Most businesspeople find themselves extremely busy, yet unproductive. It's easy to get caught up in day-to-day work, work really hard, and still miss the mark. Satisfied customers, engaged employees, and prosperous owners don't happen by chance. You must have a plan. So, why don't people plan? Maybe it seems too difficult or time-consuming.

That's the beauty of this book—it makes planning simple and fast. In an hour or so, you can create a draft of your Business Growth Plan, including your Vision, Mission, Values, Objectives, Strategies, and Priorities that fits on a single sheet of paper. An effective plan will not only improve the quality of life for all of your stakeholders, it will allow you to develop leaders throughout your organization. Most importantly, it will help you grow your business by better serving your customers, employees, and business owners.

I worked with Joe Calhoon for many years at Franklin Covey Company as we developed leaders around the world. Joe was one of our most requested consultants and highest rated keynote speakers. In the past decade since going out on his own, Joe has developed a methodology that helps business leaders plan more efficiently and effectively. The system has proven successful with hundreds of different businesses in dozens of industries.

Most businesspeople, including your competitors, don't take the time to plan well. It's a weakness for them—and an opportunity for you.

They are rightly concerned that a strategic plan will take days or weeks to develop—and who has that kind of time? Joe's book solves this problem by capturing the essence of the planning process in a way that takes about an hour of your time.

Why Should You Create a Business Growth Plan?

Before you go on a trip, you determine your destination and plan out the best route. The clearer and more exciting your destination, the greater the likelihood you will have a successful and enjoyable journey. Unfortunately, most businesses lack the joy and energy that comes with having an inspiring destination for their people. They just keep puttering along. But without planning, you lose more than an inspiring goal. Customer service droops, employees disengage, and businesses underperform. In fact, most business failures can be traced to a lack of planning.

My experience in working with businesses around the world has shown that effective organizations create their own futures through the planning process.

The One Hour Plan for Growth allows you to stop and pause for three things that are important (but unfortunately, never urgent): (1) introspection (defining what's important to you); (2) insight (understanding what's happening around you); and (3) imagination (visualizing what's possible for you).

This Planning Process Is Accessible to Everyone in an Organization

One of the fundamental problems in organizations is a lack of buy-in and engagement. As people mature in their own lives and take on greater meaning, they want significant involvement. Without involvement, there is no commitment. Involvement leads to creative contributions and employee loyalty. The involvement process is just as important as the final written plan.

The One Hour Plan for Growth encourages and allows for every employee to participate meaningfully and constructively.

Why Now?

Our world is moving at an ever-increasing speed. People want quick answers and quick fixes. But what people need are real answers and lasting solutions. This book meets people's wants *and* needs. *The One Hour Plan for Growth* provides a quick introduction to a lifelong leadership tool.

Acknowledgments

I thank God for the inspiration, wisdom, and people who helped make this book possible.

My deepest gratitude to:

- The gracious souls who have trusted our team and the business growth process. You have taught us much.
- Stephen R. Covey for an enlightening decade of learning, teaching, and applying the principles of effectiveness.
- Peter Drucker for helping me grasp the power of the planning elements.
- Jim Horan for your example and encouragement.
- Richard Narramore and the entire team at John Wiley & Sons, Inc.
- Bruce Jeffrey for helping me develop, refine, and apply the methodology that made this book possible.
- Drew Hiss, Rick Perkins, Jerry Haney, Cary Summers, Randy Reed, and Tom Cox for your ongoing contributions and encouragement.
- Case Dorman and the wonderful team at Jack Stack Barbecue.
- Rick Boxx of Integrity Resource Center for your contribution of "values" stories.
- Kyle Holt and the U, Inc. team for creating 1hour2plan.com.
- My "Gang Members"—the bike gang, the swimming gang, and the Friday morning gang—for your friendship and guidance.
- My advisory board for your courage, consideration, and wisdom.

- Della Niemuth and Megan Garringer for your outstanding service.
- My wife Diane and our son Joseph for your unconditional love, encouragement, and companionship.
- The countless others, you know who you are.

Introduction

Are You Ready to Get Started?

Here's the big idea—get your team on the same page, literally!

This book helps you create a powerful plan to grow your business on a single sheet of paper. Get ready to answer these three questions:

1. Where do you want to go? (Step 1: 25 minutes)
2. Where are you now? (Step 2: 10 minutes)
3. How will you get from here to there? (Step 3: 25 minutes)

You can do it!

In the next hour you can create a clear and compelling plan to grow your business. You will experience the clarity that leads to action and results. Are you ready to get started? If so, turn to Chapter 1 and take the shortcut.

To take the shortcut, go to Chapter 1.

If you have a little more time, a couple of hours or so, read the entire book. No matter which route you choose—in less time than most people spend talking about their need for a plan, you'll create one.

An effective growth planning system is the best indicator of whether your business will grow. It's time to develop your plan and learn a system that will serve you for the rest of your life.

No matter where your business is today, you can grow it through the system you will discover in this book. You'll also develop your own leadership skills, not through classroom training, but through the process of setting, achieving, and celebrating progress on your most important priorities.

So, what does growing a business mean for you?

- Greater job security.
- Personal wealth.
- Providing greater value for your customers.
- Creating more jobs.
- Building an extraordinary team.
- Helping people fulfill their potential.

Over the past three decades, I've had the privilege of working with hundreds of businesses and thousands of business leaders. Much of the wisdom these leaders have shared with me is included in these pages. Many of the businesses you know well—Best Buy, 3M, General Electric, and Ritz-Carlton Hotels. You'll meet other businesses and leaders for the first time in these pages.

The vast majority of this book will help you develop your plan for growth. But first, I'd like to take you on a little detour, to put the plan in perspective. I want to share some ideas that will help you live a better life *and* build a better business. If you develop an extraordinary business without living an extraordinary life, you'll miss too much. So, let's talk first about life—then business.

Now and Then, We All Need a Wake-Up Call

My wife Diane and I got married in 1983. We had our only child, Joseph, in 1984. I started my full-time speaking and consulting career in 1986. That's when I developed the habit of giving my best at the office and my leftovers to my family. I'm not proud to admit it, but it's true. I'd give the best of my service, creativity, motivation, and contributions to my profession—and my family would get whatever was left. I'd come home and announce that I was going to "veg out." In the simplest of terms, I behaved like a "couch potato" with a remote control.

About seven years into my marriage, with a six-year-old son, I experienced a life-changing encounter with a man named Drue Jennings who was president of Kansas City Power & Light and who served on 28 different boards at the time (his three children were grown). Our interaction was a serious wake-up call.

I approached Drue and told him that I wanted to be more involved in my community, and asked for his wise counsel. Drue invited me to his office and in a one-hour meeting, here's the message I heard.

Now, don't get me wrong, Drue is gracious, kind, and an effective communicator. He never said these exact words, but this is the general implication that I got.

Drue said, "So you want to be more involved in your community?" "Yes, sir," I replied. He said "Let me ask you three questions. First, are you the kind of husband you want to be?" I said, "No, sir." "Secondly, are you the kind of father you want to be?" I said, "No, sir." "Lastly, are you the kind of neighbor you want to be?" I said, "No, sir." He said, "Well, then don't worry about your community; it's people like you that screw it up in the first place."

From that day forward, I started driving into my driveway saying; "Now my most important work begins!"

Do you think I became better or worse at home because of this decision?

Do you think I became better or worse at work because of this decision?

Here's what happened on my first day, the 21st day, and the third year of my "driveway" adventure.

I remember clearly driving home that first day, repeating to myself, "Are you the kind of husband, father, and neighbor you want to be?" I had such good intentions! I somehow imagined a dramatic scenario in which my son might come running out to greet me as I pulled into the driveway. Maybe my wife would have rose petals scattered on the sidewalk, waiting in the house to say, "My man is home." I hadn't done a single thing, yet somehow I already envisioned a happy ending.

However, the first person I saw upon my arrival at home was my neighbor, Ryan. Ryan was a 120-pound second-grader with baggy shorts and a baggy T-shirt, and a chip on his shoulder as big as a railroad tie. He was being raised by a single mom. His father had left them. As I pulled into the driveway, I remember imagining Indiana Jones when he looked down into the pit of snakes, saying "Why did it have to be snakes?" I similarly mumbled to myself, "Why did it have to be Ryan?" I was committed to make the changes. But, I began realizing it wasn't going to be easy. I got out of my car and said, "Hi, Ryan." Ryan mumbled, "Hi."

Three weeks later, I couldn't get into my driveway. I had purchased a plastic basketball goal and set it up in my driveway, which was full of kids waiting for me to get home—Joseph, Ryan, two kids from across the street, two other kids from down the street, a boy and a girl from the house behind us plus another girl from around the corner. I was the commissioner, the coach, the referee, and the power forward on the team of my choice. It was great fun—and I was learning how to be a father and a neighbor.

Three years later, we celebrated Joseph's 10th birthday. The "driveway" kids and their parents were all there. I told Ryan's mom, Fran, the "driveway story"—and soon enough, she was in tears. Fran said, "You'll never realize the impact you've had on my son." I was teared up myself as I said, "You'll never realize the impact your son has had on *me*."

Since that time, I have attempted to live with a stronger sense of balance, contribution, and meaning. I want to live a better life and build a better business. How about you? Is business success enough for you?

The work that most people do is just one of many important areas of their lives. But running a business and working for a living is not the be-all and end-all to life. What good would it be if you gained the whole world and lost your soul, your family, or your health?

The point is, you don't want to make too much—or too little—of your business or your work. They are important, but they should be kept in proper perspective.

People who are truly successful—people who live truly fulfilling lives—acknowledge that their careers are an integral part of the entire picture. It's not so *un*important that they feel they can barely "tolerate" going to work, yet it's not so important that every other aspect of their lives are out of balance. Yes, there may be seasons of imbalance, but work is one of several critical areas of their lives.

Here's the cool connection: As you build a better life, you have more capacity to build a better business. As you build a better business, you have more financial resources to enjoy a better life.

Businesses are a part of life, and a person's life significantly impacts his or her career. As Ghandi said, "You can't be one person in one area of life and another person in another area of life. Life is one indivisible whole."

Here are three simple guidelines for living a better life. Identify, develop, and utilize your unique strengths and passion to bring value to other people. It's the world's greatest success principle—as you give, you receive.

Think of these three steps as:

1. Your calling
2. Your capacity
3. Your contributions

Goethe wisely observed, "The man who is born with a talent which he is meant to use, finds his greatest happiness in using it."

Live an Extraordinary Life

The history books are full of stories about men and women who were seemingly going nowhere in their lives and then achieved extraordinary results:

- Albert Einstein failed his college entrance exam. His teachers called him a misfit.
- Julia Child didn't write her famous cookbook, *Mastering the Art of French Cooking*, until she was 49. At 87, she was still cooking on PBS.
- Walt Disney failed professionally seven times before his business finally caught on.

- Oprah Winfrey, the daughter of a Mississippi sharecropper, has become one of the richest women in the world.

Here are a few more examples of people achieving extraordinary results:

- In his eighties, after writing almost 30 books, I asked Peter Drucker which book was his proudest achievement. He said, "The next one." A short time later, his next book was published.
- Louis Braille at age 15 began devising a system to help blind people read and write.
- Steven Spielberg directed *Jaws* when he was 27.
- Alexander Graham Bell invented the telephone at 29.
- Bill Gates wrote his first computer program at 13, cofounded Microsoft at 19, and became a billionaire at 31.
- Ann Landers started writing her newspaper column at 37.
- Lucille Ball debuted in the *I Love Lucy* TV show at 40.
- Sam Walton founded Walmart when he was 44.
- Dale Carnegie wrote *How to Win Friends and Influence People* at 47.
- Henry Ford created the assembly line at 50.
- Ray Kroc started McDonald's when he was 52.
- Alex Haley published *Roots* at 55.
- Col. Sanders founded Kentucky Fried Chicken when he was 65.

At his 70th birthday tribute, Zig Ziglar addressed a group of people regarding rumors of his retirement. He said, "No, I'm not going to retire, I'm going to refire! I'm not giving up, putting up, or shutting up, till I'm taken up, and quite frankly I'm just warming up." At Zig's 80th birthday celebration, he told me that he felt like some of his greatest contributions were still to come. Zig Ziglar still speaks to thousands at the time of this writing. He is 84.

You are capable of achieving extraordinary results in your life. As Eleanor Roosevelt said, "The future belongs to those who believe in the beauty of their dreams." Don't get hung up on your past. Live out of your imagination, not your memory.

I believe you were created with a unique call on your life, a capacity to develop, and contributions to make. Abraham Maslow said it this way,

"A musician must make music, an artist must paint, a poet must write if he is to be ultimately at peace with himself. What one can be, one must be." Let's explore your calling, your capacity, and your contributions.

Calling

Calling refers to vocation, employment, or a spiritual leading in your life.

You have a call in your life; we all do. Of course, if we have children, we're called to be the best parents we can be. If we're married, we're called to be the best spouses we can be. If we're neighbors, we're called to be the best neighbors we can be. You get the idea; every role comes with responsibilities. But, what about your job, your vocation, your employment?

You have a unique set of strengths and a particular passion that often points you toward your ideal vocation.

Here are three questions that can help you focus on your calling.

1. *What are your strengths?*

In their research for the book *Leaders*, Warren Bennis and Burt Nanus discovered that the top people in any organization usually get there by identifying their strengths and then focusing their efforts in the areas where they can make their greatest contribution.

Over the past several decades, I have had the privilege of conducting strengths assessments for thousands of people. Of course, it's easier to see the picture when you're outside the frame, but I'm still amazed at the unique strengths of every person I've ever met.

My friend, Rod Handley, has a nine-year-old son named Trent who is an author already—quite surprising because Trent was born with serious learning disabilities. Last Christmas, Trent interviewed me. Then he wrote and illustrated an impressive 11-page book that tells the brief story of my life. The kid's got talent—and so do you.

It can be disheartening to see people consistently devalue their own strengths. When something comes so easy to us, we have a tendency to think that it's not valuable to others, but nothing could be further from the truth.

Plato said it well: "More will be accomplished, and better, and with more ease, if every (one) does what (they are) best fitted to do, and nothing else."

Discover and value your unique strengths, as well as the strengths of others. This is one of the primary keys to building great teams and high-performing organizations.

2. *What is your passion?*

After visiting with thousands of people on this subject, I'm convinced that most people settle for the ordinary rather than pursue the extraordinary. However, that is certainly not the case with people like Dr. Gregg Raymond, Connie Suss, and Minaz Abji.

Gregg's career is dentistry; his passion is increasing people's self-confidence by providing them with a more attractive smile.

Connie Suss has owned bijin salon & spa for 25 years. Her career is as a hairdresser, and her passion is serving her customers and employees.

Minaz Abji's career is in the hospitality industry. His passion is leading teams to achieve extraordinary results.

Over the course of a lifetime, the average person will invest more than 100,000 hours in work-related activities. When people pursue their passions their vocation becomes more like a vacation.

Author Gil Baile says, "Ask yourself what makes you come alive, and go do that, because what the world needs is people who have come alive."

3. *Where can you make a good living?*

I have a good friend who has worked for the past 20 years as head of security in one of the wealthiest communities on the planet. He has served kings and queens, movie stars, presidents, and the titans of industry. I once asked him: What was the most important thing he has learned from the rich and famous? He replied without hesitation, "Money won't make you happy!" He went on to tell me that, "Many of these apparently successful individuals are some of the most miserable people on earth."

As you utilize your strengths and pursue your passion, don't "sell out" for a paycheck. You may end up miserable, too. Maybe you're miserable now. Do what you love and do it really well. You'll earn enough money to live the abundant life.

Capacity

Having flown several million miles over the past 30 years, I understand the wisdom that insists we "put on our own oxygen masks before helping others with their masks." Likewise, our contributions and rewards in life are determined by our physical vitality, the strengths we develop, our spiritual core, the quality of our relationships, and our financial well-being.

Let's explore each of these five capacities.

1. Physical
2. Mental
3. Spiritual
4. Relational
5. Financial

When any of these five capacities is neglected or distressed, you can lose your Mojo. You don't want to lose your Mojo; it's your "energy, vitality, spirit, zest, verve: power, dynamism, drive; fire, passion, ardor, zeal; informal zip, zing, pep, pizzazz, oomph, moxie, feistiness." So let's get your Mojo working.

1. *Develop your physical capacity.*

In 1969, my dad read the book *Aerobics* and took our entire family out for a 12-minute run, a fitness test. Little did I know that 30 years later, I'd be interviewing Dr. Ken Cooper, the author of the book and the man who coined the term "aerobics." Ken Cooper is a model for capacity, productivity, and genuine success.

At the time we met, Dr. Cooper was at an age when many people would have retired. Dr. Cooper was working five full-time jobs. He was a practicing physician with a full patient load, the administrator of the Cooper Clinic, a speaker who gave 150 presentations per year, a writer who had sold more than 30 million books and the chairman/chief fund-raiser for his nonprofit research center. He was almost 80 years old.

As you can imagine, Dr Cooper has physical, mental, spiritual, relational, and financial capacity that makes this all possible. Though

I am not recommending that you work five different jobs, it *does* show what's possible when you attain and maintain physical vitality.

In the years ahead, health and wellness will become increasingly important in our homes, workplaces, and society. Are you fueling your body with proper nutrition? Do you have a regular physical routine that balances endurance, strength, flexibility, coordination, and fun?

2. *Develop your mental capacity.*

Earl Nightingale, the "Dean of Personal Development," once said that if you study your profession one hour a day for three years, you will rise to the top 1 percent of your field. If you study your profession an hour a day for five years, you could become a nationally recognized expert. I've seen this happen again and again.

There is so much to learn and there are so many different ways to learn it in our Internet-based world.

Learning involves setting some realistic goals, overcoming roadblocks, sustaining motivation, and assessing your results. Learning must be accomplished in the way that works best for you. It's your choice how you will develop your unique strengths and abilities.

Are you investing the time to develop your unique strengths and abilities?

3. *Develop your spiritual capacity.*

In his book *Extraordinary* (p. 4), author John Bevere writes,

---

The truth is, God not only desires you to live extraordinarily but also has equipped you to do so . . . A remarkable, amazing, extraordinary life is not restricted to certain individuals or professions . . . but to a disposition of the heart.

Every person is unique. Every person has a spiritual dimension that houses his or her internal compass. It's the part of a person that provides a deeper meaning and purpose for his or her life. It's a connection to the Divine.

And just because this area is private, it doesn't mean that it should be neglected. Your spiritual capacity must be nurtured. As Mother Teresa said, "To keep a lamp burning we have to keep putting oil in it."

Spiritual disciplines develop extraordinary character. Business philosopher Jim Rohn says it best, "The most important question to ask on the job is not 'What am I getting?' The most important question to ask on the job is 'What am I becoming?'"

Are you investing the time to nurture your spiritual Mojo?

4. *Develop your relationships.*

It has been suggested that 90 percent of your success in life relates to your people skills. Many of our most troubling problems are relationship problems. Don Clifton teaches a powerful concept in his book, *How Full Is Your Bucket*, where he suggests that everyone has an invisible bucket and an invisible dipper. Our buckets are constantly being emptied or filled, Don says, depending on what people say or do to us. When we have a full bucket, we feel great. When our buckets are empty, we feel terrible. We use our invisible dippers to empty or fill people's buckets, based on what we say and do to other people. When we fill another person's bucket, by saying or doing things that increase his or her positive emotions, we also fill our own bucket. After I read Don's book, I started filling people's buckets. How does filling the bucket impact your work and life?

According to Gallup's research of more than 4 million employees worldwide, individuals who receive regular recognition and praise:

• Increase their individual productivity.
• Increase engagement among their colleagues.
• Are more likely to stay with their organization.
• Receive higher loyalty and satisfaction scores from customers.
• Have better safety records and fewer accidents on the job.

In his research on marriage, John Gottman found that there is a "magic ratio" of five positives to every, one negative interaction. Marriages are more likely to succeed when couples are near that five to one ratio. When there's a one-to-one ratio, marriages are more likely to end in divorce. When I learned the "magic ratio," I started bringing my wife more flowers, writing positive notes, and speaking more words of encouragement.

Are you filling the buckets of the people that matter most to you?

5. *Develop your financial capacity.*

Current statistics point out that a large percentage of people are experiencing financial hardship. No matter how much or how little a person earns, people face the challenge of living within their means.

At one time in my life, I was upside down financially. It took me seven years to pay off my debts. I know from experience that having your finances in order is good for your Mojo. It also frees up your mind to be a better employee, manager, or leader.

Financial author Robert Kawasaki teaches some valuable lessons on finance. Poor people spend all they make and remain poor, he explains. The middle-class spends their money on houses and cars and make little financial progress. Those who become rich do so by saving and investing their money first, and then living on the rest.

In *The 10 Laws of Wealth and Abundance*, author Ron Willingham writes, "Few things will block your road to wealth and abundance as will unwise borrowing."

Years ago I had the pleasure of sharing a couple hours with finance expert Sir John Templeton. He described to me in detail how he and his wife furnished their first apartment in New York City by frequenting estate sales. He said they were committed to saving and investing 20 percent of their income. Before Sir John Templeton passed away, this philanthropist became well known for his annual million-dollar gifts to those who were furthering spiritual understanding in our world.

Are you managing your money wisely? If not, where can you get some help in doing so?

Contribution

Mary Kay Ash, founder of Mary Kay Cosmetics, had the responsibility of caring for her brothers and sisters after school while her mother worked 14-hour days as a restaurant manager. Her father had tuberculosis and was an invalid most of his life, so her mother got up at 5 AM to support the family. In the afternoons, her mother would call seven-year-old Mary Kay at home with instructions on how to prepare the evening's meal.

Mary Kay was married at 17. When her husband went off to World War II, she went to work to support her three children. She didn't want to leave them at home, knowing firsthand how lonely that could be, so she took on various direct sales jobs. When her husband came home from the war, he announced that he no longer wanted to be married.

She worked the next 25 years as a saleswoman for a home products company. She retired in frustration in 1963 when yet another man she had trained was promoted above her.

During that time, Mary Kay sat down at her kitchen table to write a book that would help women survive in the male-dominated business world. She made one list that contained all the good things she'd seen in business and the other list contained the things she thought could be improved. When she looked at the lists she realized she had a great plan for a new business.

Mary Kay Cosmetics was launched in 1963. Mary Kay's motivation was to provide opportunities for women to create better lives. Today, the company has more than 1,500,000 sales consultants, and does more than $2.5 billion in annual sales.

Mary Kay built a business by giving women an opportunity that she never had. Mary Kay believes strongly in the potential of all women. She said, "Ginger Rogers did everything Fred Astaire did, but she did it backwards and in high heels."

Mary Kay Ash understood the world's greatest success principle: As you give, you receive. Many people think they have to fight to take all that they can on their way to success. The truth of the matter is—the secret to a successful, happy life is giving ourselves away. As Winston Churchill said, "We make a living by what we get; we make a life by what we give."

Just think for a moment about the people who have made the greatest impact on your life—were they takers or givers? Think of the people you know who have achieved authentic personal success, the people you respect—are they takers or givers?

I learned this lesson when I started my speaking and consulting career in the early 1980s. My first mentor was Cavett Robert, cofounder of the National Speakers Association. Each year, the NSA gives their highest award, like the Emmy or Oscar of professional speaking. It's called "The Cavett Award." The recipient is an individual who best exemplifies the caring, sharing, and giving spirit that truly was Cavett Robert. So it shouldn't surprise you that Cavett gave me the following advice to build my speaking career. He said, "If it's worth doing for fee, it's worth doing for free until people will pay you for it." So, with a couple of consulting contracts, I executed the strategy of giving myself away. I gave as many as 50 free speeches each year for several years. A decade later, I could trace virtually every piece of business I had to one of those free speeches.

You may want to consider how you could give in the various areas out of your life—your business, your family, your community. Whether you're giving your service, money, encouragement, ideas, forgiveness, energy, or anything else, ultimately as you give, you will receive.

As Cavett Robert used to say,

A bell is not a bell until you ring it.
A song is not a song until you sing it.
Love in your heart is not put there to stay;
Love is not love until you give it away.

Canadian stress management expert Hans Selye says it this way: "If you want a long life, focus on making contributions." In other words, we improve the quality and quantity of our lives as we focus on making contributions.

Here's one more thought on life. Most people dream too small. You can do extraordinary things with your life, even if you have been told differently or may believe otherwise. It will take time to implement these ideas. The good news is—you have a lifetime. So get your Mojo working.

Build an Extraordinary Business

In 1988, I had the privilege of interviewing Ewing Kauffman, one of the United States' legendary entrepreneurs. As our interview came to a close, Mr. Kauffman encouraged me to tell his story to as many people as possible. So here you go.

Mr. Kauffman started a business in his basement with $5,000. Over the next several decades, he applied proven principles and practices that helped Marion Labs create hundreds of millionaires. At the time of my interview, Mr. K., as he was lovingly called by his associates, was worth $3.2 billion. He told me that he hoped that other entrepreneurs would experience the joy of enriching people's lives as they served customers.

One of the most inspiring and memorable elements of Marion Labs' success story was a single sheet of paper entitled "Foundations For An Uncommon Company." The document was the philosophical foundation that guided the company. Everyone understood and lived by these three principles.

1. **Those who produce should share in the results.** Mr. K. told me that the two biggest mistakes that businesspeople make are: (1) they don't give their people a share of the profits, and (2) they don't give their people enough authority.
2. **Treat others the way you would like to be treated.** At Marion Labs, if you talked about someone behind his or her back, the first time you were warned, and the second time you were fired. Mr. K. said that it was a tough rule to live with, but great for morale.
3. **Give back to the community.** Mr. K. said that we owe a debt to our communities to give back with our time and money.

These three principles created a high-trust, high-performing organization like few I have ever encountered. The vision of Marion Labs was to become the most productive pharmaceutical company in the world. Productivity was measured by the gross sales and profits per associate. The company achieved its vision and set an even higher goal (which we discuss further as we "go deeper on Vision").

Mr. Kauffman's wealth has outlived him through the Kauffman Foundation. Thanks to Ewing Kauffman's generosity and foresight, his foundation is the world's largest foundation devoted to entrepreneurship and youth education.

Since that meeting almost 25 years ago, I have had the opportunity to work with hundreds of companies in a wide range of industries in various geographic locations around the world. Would it surprise you to learn that approximately 9 out of 10 businesses do not have a single sheet of paper that outlines their business plans and philosophies? Even when planning documents are created, they are often too long, unclear, and uninspiring. No wonder most business leaders consider visioning and planning activities to be a waste of time—they often *are*.

A Call to Lead

This book is a call to lead—in our organizations and in our lives. It's an attempt to narrow the gap between the way our organizations perform and the way we'd like them to perform, between the way we live our lives and the way we'd like to live our lives. It's a book about envisioning a better future and working with others to make that vision a reality.

As Warren Bennis and Burt Nanus write in their book *Leaders*, "The absence or ineffectiveness of leadership implies the absence of vision, a dreamless society, and this will result, at best, in the maintenance of the status quo or, at worst, in the disintegration of our society because of lack of purpose and cohesion."

Let's not kid ourselves—our world is becoming increasingly complex and more perilous. Leadership is becoming more challenging. Yet, the need for strong, effective, and moral leadership has never been greater. This is especially true in business. It's business that provides the value on which all other segments of society are built, the products and services that sustain life, and the wages and tax base that support education, government, nonprofits, and places of worship. If businesses don't succeed, society can disintegrate rapidly. Our future, in large part, depends on businesspeople who invest their energy and creativity to build better businesses, create more jobs, and provide value for the greater community.

Ewing Kauffman said, "All the money in the world cannot solve problems unless we work together. And, if we work together, there is no problem in the world that can stop us."

PART

Planning for Growth

CHAPTER

The Shortcut

Having an effective growth planning system is the best indicator of whether your company will grow.
—Steven S. Little, Author

Congratulations on your commitment to develop your own One Hour Plan for Growth. There are three basic ways to use this book.

1. Take the Shortcut. You'll have a plan in one hour including the **one** most important strategy to grow your business.
2. Read through the book if you want to do the in-depth version of the plan including several strategies to grow your business.
3. Involve your team in the process to create greater commitment and buy-in (see www.1Hour2Plan.com).

Think of each step in this process as a piece of your planning puzzle. At this time you don't know what the final picture will look like. As you build your plan, it may not make sense until you are done. So, you must trust the process. Let's get started. Here are the steps to the planning process.

Step 1: Where Do You Want to Go? Write Down the Long-Term Aspirations that Drive You and Your Team (25 minutes)

- 1:1 Vision Exercise—Define the big goal that will inspire you and your team (see Chapter 3).
- 1:2 Mission Exercise—Define why your organization exists, the ultimate contribution you make to your customers' lives (see Chapter 4).
- 1:3 Values Exercise—Define the standards of behavior that will help your team enjoy working together (see Chapter 5).
- 1:4 Objectives Exercise—Define the measures of your success and organizational performance (see Chapter 6).

Step 2: Where Are You Now? Write Down the Brutal Realities Facing Your Team (10 minutes)

- 2:1 Issues Exercise—Identify the big issues that must be addressed (see Chapter 7).

Step 3: How Will You Get from Here to There? Write Down the Areas of Work and Who Needs to Do What by When. (25 minutes)

- 3:1 Strategies Exercise—Define the major categories of work to be done (see Chapter 8).
- 3:2 Priorities Exercise—Define who needs to do what by when (see Chapter 9).

CHAPTER

2

An Overview of the One Hour Plan

It does not take much strength to do things, but it requires a great deal of strength to decide what to do.
—Elbert Hubbard, Philosopher and Writer

The best way to predict your future is to create it.
—Stephen R. Covey, Author

A single sheet of paper is enough to describe your organization's Vision, Mission, Values, Objectives, and Strategies, plus help focus an individual's Priorities.

As you read this book, write these six elements of your plan on the following page. See Table 2.1.

Table 2.1 Blank Template—The One Hour Plan for Growth

Priorities:

Strategies:

Vision:

Mission:

Values:

Objectives:

Business Growth Plan

Joe Calhoon

Clarity that leads to action | 10100 N. Ambassador Drive, Suite 105 / Kansas City, MO 64153 / phone: 816-285-8144 / fax: 816-285-8145 / joecalhoon.com

www.1Hour2Plan.com/resources

6

Table 2.2 Example Template—Jack Stack Barbecue

Priorities:
- Conduct meetings with six business units to communicate Vision, Mission and Values by 3/12
- Initiate use of compliment cards for management teams by 3/12
- Complete plan for City Union Mission Golf Tournament Fundraiser by 3/25

Vision:
The Nation's Premier Provider of Kansas City Barbecue.

Mission:
Creating Remarkable Barbecue Experiences.

Values:
Integrity, Respect, Passion, Positive Attitude, Excellence, Teamwork, and Service

Objectives:
- Customer Satisfaction Scores
- Employee Satisfaction Scores
- Financial Measures
- Manager/Leadership Survey Scores

Strategies:

Team Commitment: Improve employee satisfaction through consistent team engagement, positive feedback, timely performance recognition, and accountability.

Human Resources: Develop our values-driven, high performing team through effective hiring, proper placement, and ongoing training.

High Value Experience: Consistently provide exceptional value through a clean environment, a hospitable atmosphere, and extraordinary food.

Productivity: Maximize operational efficiency by utilizing available resources and technology, developing effective and scalable systems, and streamlining communication.

Marketing and Sales: Maximize sales volume by creating raving fans, increasing brand synergy/awareness, and maintaining an integrated customer contact program.

Joe Calhoon | 10100 N. Ambassador Drive, Suite 105 / Kansas City, MO 64153 / phone: 816-285-8144 / fax: 816-285-8145 / joecalhoon.com

Clarity that leads to action

Business Growth Plan

The Problems with Planning

Effective Planning strengthens people, productivity, and profitability. So, why do so few companies take the time to plan?

There are five problems with planning:

1. Most plans are too long.
2. Most planning takes too much time.
3. Too few people are engaged in planning—it's an event.
4. Many plans end up sitting on a shelf.
5. Many plans have little impact on organizational performance.

There is a better way:

- Develop a plan that fits on a single sheet of paper.
- Invest hours, not days or weeks, in the planning process.
- Engage your team in the planning process.
- Use your plan to keep on track.
- Set, achieve, and celebrate progress on priorities.

The Three-Step Planning Process

Step 1: Where do you want to go? Start by defining the long-term aspirations that drive you and your team. These include your vision, mission, and values. This builds hope. It's more important to know what big goal will inspire you and your team, what contribution you make to your customers lives, and what standards will help your team enjoy working together than having "perfect verbiage." In this first step, you will also define your measures of success, your objectives.

Step 2: Where are you now? After you know where you want to go, it's time to identify where you are now. What are the big issues that must be addressed? Identify your 5 to 10 most important issues.

Step 3: How will you get to there from here? Last, identify how you will get from where you are to where you want to go. Define the major categories of work to be done, your strategies, and who will do what by when, priorities.

That's it. The process is easy and effective. Let's get started.

If you would like to go deeper into Planning, continue reading. To take the shortcut, turn to Chapter 3.

You Have a Mountain to Climb

The experienced mountain climber is not intimidated by a mountain—he is inspired by it. The persistent winner is not discouraged by a problem—he is challenged by it. Mountains are created to be conquered; adversities are designed to be defeated; problems are sent to be solved.

—William Arthur Ward, Author

Mount Everest represents the highest achievement to climbers around the world.

In 1984, Warren Thompson envisioned a Mount Everest climb with men and women from China, Russia, and the United States. With leadership from Jim Whittaker, the first American to climb Everest, the multinational team reached the highest place in the world on Earth Day in 1990, and returned safely.

A few years after the climb, Warren Thompson participated in a three-day leadership workshop that I facilitated in Washington State. Warren and I discussed leadership and the vital role of planning. Here's the big takeaway from our conversations. Can you imagine how the climbing team might have performed had they not clearly defined the answers to these six questions? See Table 2.3.

Many businesses fail to grow because they have not clearly answered these six fundamental questions. Individuals and organizations are meant to climb, to achieve, and to make significant contributions. As you define each of these six essential elements, you will create your business growth plan.

Table 2.3 Six Questions to Engage Your Team

1. What mountain are we climbing?	Vision
2. Why are we climbing it?	Mission
3. How will we treat each other along the way?	Values
4. How will we measure our progress?	Objectives
5. What work needs to be done?	Strategies
6. Who will do what by when?	Priorities

Engage Your Team in the Planning Process

According to Gallup Research, there are three types of employees in any organization—people who are engaged, not engaged, or actively disengaged.

Only 28 percent of the workforce is engaged. These workers are the achievers (the climbers) who go the extra mile to make good things happen.

Unfortunately, the majority of the workforce (54 percent) is not engaged. These workers are the coasters (the campers) who simply put in their time.

Another group (18 percent) is actively disengaged. These workers are the destroyers (the quitters) who have given up on their highest hopes and aspirations. These people often become bitter and resentful. Their motto is, "I'm going down and I'm taking everybody with me."

Too many people live for the weekend. People live happier, healthier, and more productive lives when they live all week long. See Table 2.4.

Table 2.4 Employee Engagement

Percentage of Workforce	Gallup's Employee Descriptor	Employee Behavior	Employee Label
28%	Engaged	Go the Extra Mile	"Achievers"
54%	Not Engaged	Put in Their Time	"Coasters"
18%	Actively Disengaged	Destroy the Organization and People Around Them	"Destroyers"

In order to engage the best efforts of today's workers, it's recommended to involve your team in this planning process. You can create a plan without any involvement from your team, but you won't have as much buy-in. Here's the principle. No involvement, no commitment. Engaging your team is addressed in greater detail in Chapter 11, "What's Next?"

The Six Elements and the Three Time Frames

Your plan to grow your business does not have to be complicated. There are only six essential elements.

In your organization, the first three elements are long-term: vision, mission, and values. Once established, they remain consistent for years to come. The next two elements are mid-term: objectives and strategies. They are usually redefined every year. The last element is short-term: priorities. Priorities are defined and achieved within 30 to 90 days.

Long Term: 5 to 25 years

These elements provide the stable core around which everything else flows. "What big goal will inspire you and your team?" (Vision), "What contribution do you make to your customers' lives?" (Mission), and "What standards will help your team enjoy working together?" (Values). These first three elements of your plan tend to be timeless and foundational to all your other choices. Let's think about these first three elements and their value to your team.

Vision. Without a unifying vision, a clear destination, people will wander aimlessly with no end in mind. People will lack focus and waste time. Without one vision, you may have division. "Di" means two. You might have two visions or three. The Americans might climb one mountain, the Russians another, and the Chinese a third. Or worse yet, you might end up with a large group of people just staying at base camp giving up on the climb.

Mission. Without a mission, your team will lack common purpose. The mission of the Everest climb was to promote global understanding and environmental responsibility. Mission defines "why" you do what you do. It's your motive, your motivation. Contrary to popular belief, everyone is motivated. The bigger question is, "motivated for what purpose?" A customer-centered mission statement provides your team with the battle cry to serve your customers and thereby serve yourselves.

According to a Harris Poll of 23,000 full-time employees, only 37 percent have a clear understanding of what their organization is trying to achieve (vision) and why they are trying to achieve it (mission).

Values. What about values? Most dysfunction in a business (and all businesses have some degree of dysfunction) is a result of people problems. The root cause of these problems is related to values and behavior. Shared values set the standards for behavior that will help your team enjoy working together. How will you treat each other on your climb? Values are the answer. Values provide the foundation for building a high-trust, high-performing culture.

In summary, vision inspires, mission motivates, and values encourage people's best behavior.

Mid-Term: One to Three Years

Objectives. They are the measures of your success. Growth-focused objectives define customer measures, employee measures, and financial measures. Objectives help your team track your progress. How fast, how big, how far do you want to go in terms of customer satisfaction, employee satisfaction, revenue, profit, or any other key indicator of success?

Effective leaders understand the vital importance of objectives. What gets measured gets done. Most companies, however, do not have clearly defined, well-balanced objectives.

Strategies. In business, there are many paths you could take to achieve your vision. In marketing, for example, will you choose direct mail, e-mail campaigns, print advertising, broadcast media, referrals, convention booths, or social media? Strategies define the major categories of work to be done.

The importance of strategies is validated by a Harvard University study reported in the book, *What Really Works*. The study found that having clearly defined, well-communicated strategies is the most important element of business success.

Short Term: 30 to 90 days

Priorities. The last element of your plan is priorities. Priorities include problems to solve, goals to achieve, and capacities to develop. A business leader recently told me that his team had worked for weeks to create a plan. The plan was about 100 pages long. Once the plan was written, it sat on a shelf. The plan was missing an important element, priorities.

Without priorities there will be little progress. Priorities define who does what by when. See Table 2.5.

Table 2.5   The One Hour Plan for Growth

The Three Time Frames	The Six Elements	The Six Elements Defined
Long Term 5–25 Years	Vision	**What big goal will inspire your team?** • How good do you want to be at providing what to whom on what geographic scale? • Is your vision clear and inspiring?
	Mission	**What contribution do you make to your customers' lives?** • What's your purpose? • Will it fit on a T-shirt?
	Values	**What standard will help your team enjoy working together?** • Do they arouse your highest degree of effort, proficiency, and character?
Mid-Term 1–3 Years	Objectives	**How will you measure success?** • Are your objectives growth-focused? • Are you measuring customer satisfaction, employee satisfaction, and financial success? • Are they clear and simple?
	Strategies	**What are the major categories of work to be done?** • Do you have a clear end in mind for each of these strategic categories? • What strategic choices will help you address your issues?
Short Term 30–90 Days	Priorities	**Who will do what by when?** • Do your priorities start with a verb, end with a date, and have something measurable in between? • Is each priority assigned to a person?

Let's create a clear and simple plan to grow your business. I know this will confront some people's need for detail. You can get the details later. Let's start with clarity and simplicity.

Jack Welch said, "You can't believe how hard it is for people to be simple, how much they fear being simple. They worry that if they're simple, people will think they're simple-minded. In reality, of course, it's just the reverse."

Your team has a mountain to climb. Effective leaders understand that the six elements must be clearly defined to engage the best efforts of your team and optimize your organization's performance.

As you read through this book, you develop a clear and compelling plan to grow your business, focus on what's important, develop leadership capacity, get everyone on the same page, and help people become more successful.

It takes as much energy to wish as it does to plan. So, why not plan?

We've rarely seen a business plan that was too short. We have seen hundreds that would make an acceptable cure for insomnia. Here's the good news—we have never encountered a business that couldn't fit their plan on a single sheet of paper. Sure, you have to cut out a lot of verbiage, but getting the plan on a single sheet of paper forces you to become really clear about what's important.

As you read this book, you learn a powerful planning system that can serve you and your organization for years to come.

Most Organizations Don't Have a Planning Process

Plans are nothing; planning is everything.

—Dwight D. Eisenhower,
34th President of the United States

General Eisenhower was the Supreme Commander of the D-Day invasion on June 6, 1944. "Ike" had a major role in planning the assault on Hitler's "Fortress Europe." The massive invasion included air, sea, and land operations. For example, the plan included 12,000 planes, more than 5,000 ships (from battleships to landing craft) and 130,000 troops landed on 50 miles of beach in Normandy. Needless to say, the original plan needed to be altered as the battle progressed. Eisenhower understood that, "Plans are nothing; planning is everything."

The same principle holds true for your business—developing a "plan" is where you begin. Here are six proven "planning" process steps that will take any organization to the next level.

1. Develop a business growth plan that fits on a single sheet of paper. (You can certainly include greater detail on additional pages.)
2. Set priorities to be accomplished in the next 30–90 days.
3. After 30–90 days celebrate progress, review the plan and set new priorities for the next 30–90 days.
4. Continue this process until the end of the year.
5. When the New Year begins, develop a new business growth plan that fits on a single sheet of paper.
6. Repeat steps 2 to 5.

This process of planning, achieving, and celebrating your progress is powerful in its simplicity and effectiveness.

Case Study: Jack Stack Barbecue–Using a Growth Plan to Take a Business to the Next Level

Jack Stack Barbecue was founded in 1974 by Jack Fiorella. Jack grew up in his dad's barbecue business from the time he was old enough to wash dishes. Jack Stack's original Martin City location seated 65 customers. From 1987 to 1997 company revenues tripled. From 1997 to 2008 revenues increased by another 600 percent. Today, Jack Stack Barbecue operates four full-service restaurants, a catering company, and a shipping division that ships their products nationwide.

If you stopped reading now, you would get the wrong impression about Jack Stack Barbecue. You see, Jack Stack Barbecue isn't a company that is primarily concerned with more stores, customers, and dollars. This company is all about a unique approach to business and it's the company's way of doing business that has produced its impressive results. As you read the Jack Stack Barbecue story throughout this book, I believe you will be challenged to take your business to the next level. But it all starts with the way you think about business and people and your growth plan.

Here's a little company history from Jack Stack's president, Case Dorman. Later in the book you will hear from other members of the management team.

JOE: What's the essence of the Jack Stack Barbecue story?

CASE: Our story is about a company that is passionate about serving. We love what we do, we love our team, and we want our people to be successful.

JOE: You remind me of a brief conversation I once had with Bill Marriott at the Marriott Marquis in New York City. He said, "If we take care of our people, they'll take care of the customers and that will take care of the bottom line."

What are the other philosophies that guide Jack Stack Barbecue?

CASE: The leadership piece is especially important in the service industry. We're in the people business. We're in the business of developing people and helping them understand the benefits of serving and providing for other people. If we do that really well for our employees, and we need great leaders to do that, we can be very successful.

JOE: One of the reasons that we chose Jack Stack Barbecue as a case study is because there is both a product and service component to your business.

CASE: It's really more than that. We refer to it as an experience. We have to have great product. We have to have great service. But, what you really want is an experience. When you come into Jack Stack Barbecue, whether you are a regular customer that dines with us once a week or somebody traveling through town, we want the customers to say, "Wow!"

JOE: Tell us about how the business started.

CASE: My wife's grandfather, Russ Fiorella, had a number of neighborhood grocery stores in Kansas City. In 1957 when his son, Jack Fiorella, was a teenager, they opened the original Smokestack

Barbecue on South 71 Highway in Kansas City. Jack helped his dad from day one and learned all the responsibilities. Jack did that from 1957 until 1974. He was 32 years old when he left.

JOE: That's when he opened the Martin City location?

CASE: That's right. He wanted to make his own life. Over time, the Martin City location became quite successful. Then, in 1979 Jack set out to expand his concept. The strange thing is he opened it about 15 blocks away from the most successful restaurant we have right now. But, it was during a recession with 18 percent interest rates and all kinds of economic troubles. The business just couldn't make it. The cost of financing was overwhelming the company and Jack closed the location two years later. This was an important time in Jack's life. Adversity always reveals the true character of a person. Jack made a commitment to come back to the Martin City store and redouble his efforts. He came back with a lot of drive, energy, and focus to rebuild the Martin City business. It soon became one of the most popular and successful restaurants in south Kansas City.

JOE: When my family and I moved to Kansas City in 1986, we first started making a 30-minute drive to experience Jack Stack Barbecue.

CASE: Jack, my mother in law, Delores, my brother in law, Kevin Fiorella, and my wife, Jennifer, were working very hard at that time to create a new type of barbecue restaurant. Taking the concept and adding much more diversity to the menu and improving the service standards and the atmosphere to create a full service barbecue dining experience.

JOE: Is this when you started expanding again?

CASE: Yes. A few years later, in 1991 we were attending a lot of catering and banquet events in the city. We were continually dismayed by the poor quality of catered food. We would constantly talk to each other about it. We just knew we could do a better job than others with catered food. So we set out to open our own catering division. Today, it's one of the largest restaurant-owned catering companies in the country.

JOE: What happened next?

CASE: We decided we would take on a second location. That happened in 1997. That was a big step for us because it meant spreading out our resources, our team, and our family. How do you make that transition from individual family owned business to a multi-unit operator? And, do it well? Most people do not do it well and a few do it very well. We realized there were some key elements.

We had to quit thinking like an independent restaurant operator. Restaurants tend to be chef-driven or systems-driven. To grow, we needed to be systems-driven.

We had to start thinking and acting more like a business in the way we developed our people, shared information, and made decisions.

We had to capture the culture we had developed through all the years in Martin City and bring it to the new business locations.

That's where our first mission statement was born. We wanted to define and communicate what we were about as a company so that new team members could buy-in to our culture.

JOE: What other growth challenges did you experience?

CASE: It was becoming harder and harder to compete for the best people. Because I had been on the restaurant frontlines working at other restaurants, I understood what the staff was going through and their challenges. I came to the company in 1987 as the general manager of Martin City. So my goal at the time was to create a restaurant where, if you were a professional in the food services industry in Kansas City, you would want to work for us.

JOE: You had a lot of competition at this time.

CASE: Yes. In the mid-1990s the national chains were coming into the marketplace and it was getting much more difficult to compete for the best people. They were able to pay more than we were paying. They were able to offer benefits that we were not able to offer. They were able to do things for their staff that we couldn't afford to do for our staff. We realized that we were either going to have a long hard road as an independent, trying to differentiate ourselves from these national chains. Probably never being able to offer the kind of opportunities they offered to their staff or we needed to get in the game with them and be able to compete with them on a similar level.

JOE: You became more competitive in terms of hiring the best people.

CASE: Exactly. We had to adapt to the changing marketplace. We began to offer health insurance in 1997. The next year we picked up dental and life insurance. In 1999 we began our 401(k) program. Up to that point we didn't even have an official vacation policy. Now, we have an employee emergency program that is funded voluntarily by our employees. So, if employees are in a financially distressed situation, they can come to a group of their peers and request a grant that they don't have to pay back. It's a gift from their co-workers.

JOE: Let's get into your planning process. What benefits have you experienced from the planning process over the past several months?

CASE: I am experiencing a clearer direction in my day. It allows me to get up and be productive from the earliest part of my day. As I go through the week, it gives me something to refocus my energy. Because the restaurant business is really driven by a constant flow of urgent items, it's really important for us to be able to stop, go back, and revisit what the plan was for the week. What was to get accomplished for the week? And then, reengage and make sure we get that done.

JOE: The restaurant business can be very urgency-driven, making it hard for management to stay focused on their plan and priorities. A lot of restaurants, a lot of businesses, are driven by the urgent and lose focus on what's important.

CASE: That's right. Having a plan helps me stay focused on what's important. You have talked to some of our managers; we're all experiencing a renewed sense of clarity and focus.

Here are verbatim comments from various Jack Stack managers regarding the process of developing and implementing their business growth plans.

What is the process like for you and your team?

- It has given me the confidence that I can achieve more by using these "tools."
- We are accomplishing more, as individuals and teams.
- We are celebrating our progress.
- I am clear about what I should be doing.
- We are creating a culture that is inspiring to be a part of.
- Great experience, easy to understand, very clear and to the point.

- It was simple and provided focus and clarity about who we are and where we are going as a business.
- Enlightening . . . it has opened my eyes to the big picture.
- I have a clear understanding of what I want my team to accomplish.
- We have refocused and recommitted to our guests and employees.
- I am more effectively growing my staff and my managers to deliver great guest experiences.
- Creating our business plan has helped create tangible priorities to grow our business.
- All of our objectives and priorities are achievable and people understand the importance of them.
- I see this as a long-distance race, not a sprint.
- The team feels more included and informed.
- I've been able to move the urgent and not important tasks out of my day.
- It was challenging to pinpoint what Jack Stack means to *all* employees.
- Exciting and eye-opening.
- I have a new resolve for success with a plan to achieve it.

When asked if the process was working, all 18 managers replied "yes." Then, we asked why is it working?

- Involvement, ownership to all individuals—no one person.
- It's simple and easy to understand.
- We're on the same page.
- It has unified the team around what we are trying to accomplish.
- It has helped us achieve more by setting clear priorities related to what's important.
- It's a simple, structured, step-by-step process.
- It has definitely helped me become a better manager.
- Simplicity and clarity—it doesn't feel like we're loaded down— we have a vision and a plan to get us there.
- Everyone enjoys being involved.
- There is nothing "hokey" or "gimmicky."

PART

Where Do You Want to Go?

CHAPTER

Vision

What Big Goal Will Inspire You and Your Team?
(6 minutes)

Good business leaders create a vision, articulate the vision, passionately own the vision, and relentlessly drive it to completion.
—Jack Welch, Former Chairman and CEO, General Electric

The true motivator for employees is the spirit of cooperation that comes with a shared vision.
—Greg Bustin, Author

Where there is no vision, the people perish.
—King Solomon

A vision is a concise word picture of your organization's ideal future. Your vision should be measurable, achievable, and inspiring.

Wilson Auctioneers

Wilson Auctioneers has sold the boyhood home of Bill Clinton and thousands of other assets from their headquarters in Hot Springs, Arkansas. During a team meeting with Wilson Auctioneers, Joe Wilson leaned back in his chair, looked to the ceiling, and said, "You know what I really want us to become?" After a long pause, he continued, "I want us to be the finest real estate auctioneers in Arkansas." That was it. That was their vision. It was inspired and inspiring. Wilson Auctioneers measures their success in terms of market share and customer satisfaction. The entire team resonated with the vision and developed a plan to make it a reality. Over the next year, the team at Wilson Auctioneers doubled their revenues while maintaining high levels of customer satisfaction.

Why Create a Vision?

A vision communicates what you want your organization to become. The creation of a vision provides:

- A clear and compelling picture of your ideal future.
- Criteria for strategic decision making.
- Inspiration for higher levels of contribution and performance.
- A compass that points you in the right direction.

How to Write a Vision Statement

You can write a clear and concise vision statement by answering four fundamental questions:

1. How good do you want your organization to be? For example, do you want to have the highest revenues, most impressive customer satisfaction, best quality products/service, and so forth?
2. What are you providing, in terms of specific products and services?
3. Which customers and markets do you serve?

4. What is the geographic scope of your business—from your immediate neighborhood to the world?

Once you answer these questions, you can wordsmith your vision statement. The big idea here is to be able to answer them with absolute clarity, focus, and simplicity.

Here are a couple examples:
Z3 Graphix in Lenexa, Kansas
See Table 3.1.

Table 3.1

1. Inspiring Picture of Your Position in Your Marketplace:	"The premier provider of
2. Products and Services:	innovative direct marketing solutions
3. Customers and Markets:	to businesses
4. Scope:	in the Midwest."

Batts Communications in Raytown, Missouri
See Table 3.2.

Table 3.2

1. Inspiring Picture of Your Position in Your Marketplace:	"The trusted provider of
2. Products and Services:	telecom solutions
3. Customers and Markets:	for the small and medium-size companies
4. Scope:	in Kansas City."

Once you get this far, you'll want to follow the "good enough" principle. In other words, it's "good enough" for this stage in your planning process as long as you can say, "That's what I want us to become." You can always refine your language at a later time. For example, you might want to shorten your vision and say, "Kansas City's trusted provider of telecom solutions."

Examples of Vision Statements

Here are some well-written vision statements.

To be the Worldwide Airline of Choice.
—Delta Airlines

North America's premier source for redemption and incentive merchandise.
—Redemption Plus

The Region's leader in automotive excellence.
—Randy Reed Automotive Group

Kansas City's finest salon and spa experience—every day.
—bijin salon & spa

To be the world's premier food company, offering nutritious, superior tasting foods to people everywhere.
—Heinz

The World's preferred provider of select Southern pine through sustainable growth.
—Barge Forest Products

To dominate the global food-service industry.
—McDonald's

To be the world's leading diabetics care company.
—Novo Nordisk

The Nation's leader in innovative railing systems.
—Livers Bronze Company

Apple is committed to bring the best personal computing products and support to students, educators, designers, scientists, engineers, business persons, and consumers in over 140 countries around the world.
—Apple

Exercise 1:1 Write Your Vision Statement

Now it's time to write your vision statement. Simply follow the four-step process by answering the questions:

1. How good do you want to be? (Be realistic. Your goal must be attainable.)
2. At providing what? (Identify what products and services you provide.)
3. To whom? (Focus on your ideal customers and markets.)
4. On what type of scale? (Define a realistic geographic area in which you can excel.)

You want to use your own words as you complete this. Here are some examples to prompt your thinking. See Table 3.3.

Table 3.3

The Four Questions	Words You Might Use	Write Your Own
How good do you want to be? (Inspiring picture of your position in the market)	• Leading • Most productive • Highest quality • Largest	"The _____ provider (How will you measure it?)
At providing what? (Products and services)		of _____
To whom? (Customers and markets)	• Women • Homeowners • High-net-worth individuals • Small business owners	to _____ _____
On what type of scale? (Geographic scope)	• Metro area • Region • Country • World	in _____ _____."

(continued)

(*continued*)

Write your vision statement and transfer it to your business growth plan.

_____

_____

_____

_____

_____

Congratulations!

You have completed 10 percent of your business planning process.

If you would like to go deeper on your Vision Statement, continue reading.

To take the shortcut, go to Chapter 4.

Case Study: Jack Stack Barbecue Vision—The Big Goal that Inspires Our Team

JOE: How did you develop your initial mission statement in 1997?

CASE: I wrote what I thought it should be. It wasn't like I was reading books about mission statements and decided to write it; I was just trying to help our team understand who we were and how we got to where we were. I wanted to say it as succinctly and simply as possible, so that we'd have something we could rally around and measure ourselves against. Our initial mission was:

To treat our team with respect, our guests as family, and to offer the finest barbecue experience in the country.

JOE: Did your initial mission statement serve you well?

CASE: It did. We were able to sustain and develop our culture in multiple locations as we grew our company. We shared the mission statement with new employees during orientation, and continually reinforced it during all of our company meetings.

JOE: Why did you decide to write separate vision, mission, and values statements?

CASE: The initial statement was actually too long; people couldn't remember it or recite it. And since it also included elements of vision, mission, and values, we decided to write separate statements that would be clearer, more compelling, and more memorable.

JOE: Let's talk about your new vision: "The Nation's Premier Provider of Kansas City Barbecue." Tell me about what those words mean to you, and how you developed them.

CASE: I looked to the future—25 years from now, 50 years from now— and thought about what I wanted our organization to be. What stood out to me was that we would be the best in class, best in our industry, and strive for the highest level of performance possible in our segment of upscale casual dining. The national focus was a by-product of the understanding that we currently have a national brand. We ship to the continental U.S., and we've catered to 15 different states in the country. We want to continue to grow that national presence in the coming years.

JOE: Tell me about "Kansas City Barbecue."

CASE: Kansas City Barbecue offers a very specific style of barbecue for which we're famous—one that's done on an open wood-fired brick oven. We are also known for barbecuing different kinds of meat, beef, pork, poultry, lamb, even seafood. Kansas City–style sauce is tomato-based; most are sweet and/or tangy.

JOE: How is that different from the barbecue in other parts of the country?

CASE: The best-known region for barbecue in the country is Texas, which is predominately a beef barbecue. Memphis is traditionally a pork barbecue with either a dry rub or sauced option; and the Southeast, such as the Carolinas is also known for pork barbecue, usually with a vinegar-based sauce. So, we don't want to be the best Southeastern- and Carolina-style barbecue, the best Texas-style barbecue, or the best Memphis-style barbecue, we want to be the best Kansas City– style barbecue. This is an essential, differentiating part of our vision.

JOE: Is there anything else about the vision that is important to you?

CASE: Yes. We purposely made it so that it doesn't say anything about how many locations we want to have, having the most people served, or making the most money. We feel that being best in class is about having the highest quality product and service, and delivering a great experience.

The Best Visions Are Measurable

How would you like to attend a basketball game where no one kept score, or watch a golf tournament without knowing the players' standings? Not much point, is there? Not much fun either.

—Jerry Haney, *Making Culture Pay*

Legendary Kansas City–based Marion Labs, founded by Ewing Kauffman, wanted to be the "most productive" pharmaceutical company in the world. They measured "productive" based on sales and profits per associate. Since their competitors were public companies, figures like revenue, profits, and numbers of employees were public knowledge. It was an effective and easy measurement—and they achieved it.

Jerry Haney, a former Marion executive, told me that they added another BHAG (Big Hairy Audacious Goal). They wanted to grow profits by 50 percent per year for five years. That goal was also achieved.

"Measurable" means you have defined a meaningful goal; there is a specific number everyone is aiming for; you'll know when you've arrived and you'll know how you're progressing. Examples include:

- Gross revenue
- Percent increase in revenue
- Profit
- Percent increase in profit
- Revenues and/or profit per employee
- Customer satisfaction

Of course, your vision should also be achievable—meaning that it can be done with extraordinary effort, effectiveness, and efficiency. In other words, it's challenging, but not impossible.

Three Criteria for an Effective Vision Statement

Simplify (the) complex world into a single organizing idea, a basic principle or concept that unifies and guides everything.

—**Jim Collins**, *Good to Great*

Wilson Auctioneers' vision was so effective because it met three criteria:

1. It's what they did best.
2. It's what they were passionate about.
3. It drove their financial performance.

These three elements provide useful criteria for businesses and individuals trying to clarify the unique contributions they want to make to our world.

In his book, *Good to Great*, Jim Collins suggests that you build a life around three criteria:

- Work for which you have a genetic or God-given talent and perhaps you could become one of the best in the world in applying that talent.
- You are doing work you are passionate about and absolutely love to do.
- You are well paid for what you do.

At the intersection of these three criteria, individuals and organizations find fulfillment and success.

Collins concludes that the simplicity found at the intersection of these three questions helps make companies "great." I once asked Jim Collins if he believed that companies could be "great" by being the best in their geographic area. He said, "Absolutely." In other words, you may have a vision "To be the best dry cleaning business in southeast Kansas City"—and that's great!

But how do you measure being the "best?" How will you know when you've arrived? The answer may lie in your revenues, profit, customer satisfaction, market share—or other measures you choose.

The Man on the Moon

As a young boy in the early 1960s, I remember John Kennedy challenging our country with an inspiring vision: "We will take a man to the moon and return him to earth safely by the end of the decade. We do it, not because it is easy, but because it is hard." I was inspired. I was engaged. I eagerly anticipated and paid attention to every launch into space. Then, in 1969, just before the end of the decade, I watched on television as Neil Armstrong walked on the moon.

Vision provides direction. Like a rudder on a ship, it guides your forward progress. Thomas Edison said, "Genius is 1 percent inspiration and 99 percent perspiration." Vision is that 1 percent of inspiration—the end in mind that precedes the perspiration, the work you do, the results you accomplish.

People May Think You're Crazy

Of all the things I've done, the most vital is coordinating the talents of those who work for us and pointing them toward a certain goal.

—Walt Disney

Walt Disney reserved Saturday mornings to spend time with his family. One day, while sitting watching his two daughters play on the merry-go-round, he had a vision. In his imagination, he saw a family park where families could enjoy playing together. Not just any park, a $17 million park on 18 acres. When he shared his idea with others, most people thought he was out of his mind.

But in the 1950s, Walt Disney decided to sell his Palm Springs vacation home, borrowed $100,000 against a life insurance policy, and started raising money to make this vision a reality. He explained, "I've only thought of money in one way, and that is that it's something you use to do something *with*. I plow back everything I make into the company. I look at it this way: If I can't use the money now, if I can't have fun with it, I'm not going to be able to take it with me."

Disneyland opened to the public on July 18, 1955. Since that time, the park has been visited by more than 600 million guests—including presidents, royalty, and other heads of state. Disney's vision is a reality.

Plenty of people outside your business with whom you share your ideas may well think you're crazy. But as long as your team believes in and is committed to the vision, all these naysayers will do is to provide the motivation to do the "impossible."

The Customer-Centered Mission Statement

What Contribution Do You Make to Your Customers' Lives? (6 minutes)

A mission statement is defined as "a long awkward sentence that demonstrates management's inability to think clearly." All good companies have one.
—Scott Adams, *The Dilbert Principle*

Making a distinctive difference in the lives of individuals and society is the mission—the organization's purpose and very reason for being.
—Peter Drucker, Father of Modern Management

The Ritz-Carlton is a place where the genuine care and comfort of our guests is our highest mission.
—Ritz-Carlton Mission Statement

A mission statement is a clear and compelling statement of why your organization exists. A good mission defines the ultimate benefit, the unique contribution you make to your customers' lives.

Henry Ford—A Man with a Mission

Henry Ford formed the Ford Motor Company in 1903. By 1907, it was one of about 30 automobile manufacturers in the United States. Ford had captured 15 percent market share when he declared his mission: "[To] build a motor car for the great multitude . . . It will be so low in price that no man making a good salary will be unable to own one and enjoy with his family the blessing of hours of pleasure in God's great open spaces . . . everybody will be able to afford one, and everyone will have one."

This inspiring customer-centered mission statement ignited the creative energy of Ford's design team. Within a couple decades, Ford Motor Company became the market leader. However, growing a business of this magnitude certainly came with challenges.

In 1913, Ford hired 963 people for every hundred employees that stayed on the payroll. On January 5, 1914, he announced a radical change in compensation. Workers would no longer receive $2.38 for a nine-hour day; they would be paid $5 for an eight-hour day, plus profit sharing. After this change was established, profits rose from $30 million in 1914 to $60 million in 1916; in other words, they *doubled* over a two-year period.

Increases in productivity from the assembly line then enabled Ford to dramatically cut the price of the Model T. The Model T sold for $825 in 1908, but by 1913, one could be purchased for $99. Henry Ford's mission became a reality; and to this day, families around the world "are enjoying the blessings of hours of pleasure in God's great open spaces"—thanks to Ford's customer-centered mission statement.

Why Create a Mission Statement?

A mission communicates an organization's reason for being. Mission provides:

- A powerful statement of your purpose—it tells your employees and customers *why* you do what you do.

- Motivation for your staff by defining your primary motive, the value you provide for your customers.
- An anecdote for the dreary day-to-day grind that consumes many lives.
- A tool to stay focused on what's important—serving your customers.

Examples of Mission Statements

Here are some well-written Mission Statements.

To organize the world's information and make it universally accessible and useful.

—Google

Providing freedom and independence to people with limited mobility.

—The Scooter Store

Creating memories that last a lifetime.

—Cruise Holidays of Kansas City

To nourish and delight everyone we serve.

—Darden Restaurant Group

Better vision for a better life.

—HBR Optometrists

Helping our customers find more customers.

—Z3 Graphix

To make people who are away from home feel they are among friends and really wanted.

—Marriott Hotels

Exercise 1:2 Write Your Own Customer-Centered Mission Statement

We've made it really simple for you to get started on this exercise. First, think about the value you provide to your customers, and simply fill in the blank. Your mission could start with the words, "Helping our customers . . ."—and then all you have to do is complete the statement. For example, an investment company may write: "Helping our customers build wealth through wise counsel." Table 4.1 shows some examples that might help you create your mission statement.

Table 4.1

Car Dealership	Helping our customers choose the ideal vehicle.
Wellness Health Provider	Helping our customers enjoy better health.
Shipping Company	Helping our customers satisfy their shipment and delivery needs.
Travel Company	Helping our customers experience the joy of travel and adventure.
Insurance Company	Helping our customers be relieved of insurable financial risks.
Music Store	Helping our customers express and enjoy their musical passion.
Rental Car Company	Helping our customers enjoy a stress-free experience with a safe and dependable vehicle.
Utility Company	Helping our customers enjoy a higher quality of life with safe, clean, and reliable energy.
Recreational Vehicle Company	Helping our customers enjoy the world's highways, destinations, and people.
Grocery Store	Helping our customers enjoy a quality shopping experience and all they purchase.
Plumbing Company	Helping our customers clean up the mess and get it working again.

Write your mission statement and transfer it to your business
growth plan.

_____

_____

_____

_____

_____

Congratulations!

You have completed 20 percent of your business planning process.
    If you would like to go deeper on your Mission Statement,
continue reading.
    To take the shortcut, go to Chapter 5.

Case Study: Jack Stack Barbecue–The Customer-Centered Mission

JOE: When I worked with Stephen Covey throughout the 1990s, there
was a lot of confusion in the marketplace about mission statements.
Many people would refer to a mission statement as an organization's vision, mission, and values. Your original mission statement
included these three elements.
    Peter Drucker, on the other hand, referred to mission as pur-
pose. He suggested a mission statement should be 10 words or less.
Now, you have a four-word mission statement. I think Peter
Drucker would be impressed.

CASE: Our mission is "Creating Remarkable Barbecue Experiences." It
is only four words, but those words mean a lot to our staff. We've
found as we've gone through this exercise with the stores that "creating" has proven to be a word that the staff really likes. "Creating"
provides our staff with a strong sense of ownership—since they are
the ones who do the creating.

JOE: How do you reinforce that sense of ownership and your mission
throughout the organization?

CASE: We hear comments throughout the day, and we also receive notes from our customers. It's funny how many "remarkable barbecue experience" remarks we get. We use an online "Daily Notebook" system into which all the managers feed positive comments. Additionally, our people check their work against our mission—and that provides the greatest value. Our employees are constantly asking themselves, "Am I creating a remarkable barbecue experience?"

JOE: Who are some of the people asking this question?

CASE: It's everyone. It's the pit master who operates the barbecue ovens and prepares thousands of pounds of product to serve that day, and is asking himself: Does each piece of product that he pulls from that barbecue oven qualify for creating a remarkable barbecue experience? It's the line cooks who are preparing the plate by cutting the product and placing it on the plate; are *they* creating that experience as well? It's also the prep cook who is hand-breading the onion rings or the deep-fried mushrooms that we're going to serve our customers. He has to ask: Are we using the freshest produce? Is our batter perfect? Are we doing the kind of work that's going to create a remarkable barbecue experience?

It's the dishwasher who's washing the pots and pans and presenting a clean and sanitary environment, dishes and silverware, so that our guests can have nothing less than a remarkable barbecue experience. It's the host and hostess who greet you at the front door and make that first impression and provide an introduction— or give you a great farewell and thanks for being here that completes the remarkable barbecue experience.

And, obviously, it's the server who is going to touch every guest that we have and make sure that our timing is perfect, and that each guest is provided everything they need to truly have that remarkable experience.

One of the things that we initiated many years ago was a role we call the *expeditor*, who is always a member of management from our restaurant. We have multiple checks throughout the process wherein we make sure that the plate on its way out to the dining room is perfect. But the last checkpoint is always the expeditor—he or she puts their stamp of approval on that order. They ensure that it is the right order, that it's hot, it's fresh and perfectly prepared.

JOE: What exactly does the word "remarkable" mean to you and your company?

CASE: Remarkable, as we have discussed with our team and amongst ourselves, means outstanding, exceptional, excellence, as well as an experience worth commenting about—something that you just felt *compelled* to discuss or share.

JOE: What about the words "barbecue experience"?

CASE: Barbecue is about what we do in the truest sense of the word; we offer the most diverse barbecue menu in the country. We barbecue traditional favorites in addition to seafood, poultry, lamb, vegetables, and our hickory pit beans. Barbecue is the focus of all the things that we do—the many different ways to experience barbecue. You can experience it by dining at one of our restaurants, or by having us come to your home or business and cater an event for you. You can experience it by ordering products to be shipped to your aunt or uncle or loved one across the country, and then get the chance to try the product and love it. So that's where the experiences came in.

JOE: And you reinforce your vision, mission, and values by telling stories.

CASE: People remember stories. Just last week I was in Mystic, Connecticut with Todd and Andrea Hulse, who run our catering business. We were doing the prep work for a catering event feeding 3,000 people at the commissioning of the USS *Missouri*. The three of us were having breakfast in a local restaurant, and one of the customers in the restaurant noticed Todd's Jack Stack Barbecue jacket. The man's son said, "Look dad, Jack Stack." The dad introduced himself and said, "Jack Stack is my favorite restaurant in the world. I used to go to Lenexa, Kansas, to do business. Now one of my primary reasons for going to Kansas is the Jack Stack Barbecue." It was a pretty incredible moment, because that's exactly why our organization exists. Our mission is, "Creating Remarkable Barbecue Experiences." And I got to see that we were indeed doing just that.

Does Your Mission Fit on a T-Shirt?

Peter Drucker, known as the "Father of Modern Management," once told the story of a group of health-care professionals who developed a mission statement for the emergency room that read. "Our mission is healthcare." Short, yes; but not so clear and compelling. After further discussion, the administrators acknowledged that the emergency room actually did not take care of health; it took care of patients' illnesses or injuries. After discussing it further, they realized that the true purpose of the emergency room was to give patients and their loved ones assurance, even if the workers couldn't give them immediate health care. So they created another mission statement: "To give assurance to the afflicted." This mission makes the priority for nurses and doctors to see every new patient within one minute of their arrival, "to give assurance."

Peter Drucker also suggests that you put your mission to something he calls the "T-shirt test"; in other words, can your entire mission fit on a T-shirt? Is it 10 words or less? Does it describe why your organization exists? Does it provide direction for doing the right things? If you can't recite your mission as quickly as your phone number, then it's too long. Keep at it; you'll get there.

Every Organization Has a Mission Statement

In *The Mission Statement Book* author Jeffrey Abrahams suggests that the first mission statement may have been recorded in Genesis, with the command "Be fruitful and multiply." One of contemporary culture's best-known mission statements comes from *Star Trek*, "Space, the Final Frontier . . . These are the voyages of the Starship Enterprise. Its five-year mission: To explore strange new worlds, to seek out new life and new civilizations, to boldly go where no man has gone before."

Whether an organization acknowledges it by posting it on the wall or not, it has a mission statement. Some mission statements are written and widely shared. Other mission statements are unwritten and left to the imagination.

Mission is purpose. It's why you do what you do. It's your motive, your motivation. The purest motives involve serving others. When you serve others, you best serve yourself.

I've asked thousands of people what the purposes of their businesses are, and I'm sure it won't surprise you to hear that the number one answer is, "To make money." Often people tell me that the mission of their business is simply to make money for the owner.

More and more people are beginning to understand that the mission of every successful company *should* be to serve customers. There is nothing to be ashamed of with a customer-centered mission, it's a rally cry to succeed and prosper.

Creating Memories that Last a Lifetime

Mark and Mimi Comfort bought a Cruise Holidays franchise almost 20 years ago. Shortly thereafter, Mark, Mimi, and their team developed a wonderful mission statement: Creating memories that last a lifetime. And that's exactly what they do. Customers cruise the rivers of Europe, the Amazon, the Far East, the Mediterranean, Alaska, and the Caribbean—all while creating memories that last a lifetime.

In *The Essential Drucker*, a spectacular compilation of Peter Drucker's work, he writes, "That business *purpose* and business *mission* are so rarely given adequate thought is perhaps the single most important cause of business frustration and business failure. Conversely, in outstanding businesses . . . success always rests to a large extent on raising the question, what is our business? . . . and on answering it thoughtfully and thoroughly."

You'll want to invest some time here. But you don't want to *waste* time.

Integrating Your Belief System and Your Business

Privately held Fortune 500 company, ServiceMaster strives to be a "Christian" company. Currently based in Memphis, Tennessee, the organization has more than 5,500 company-owned and franchise locations and employs 32,000 people. It was founded as a moth-proofing company in 1929 by Marion E. Wade, a former minor league baseball player, life insurance salesman, and door-to-door salesman. In 1942, Wade sold his first franchise license for his residential and commercial on-site carpet cleaning business.

However, Wade experienced a significant turning point in his personal life and his business two years later. He was badly burned in an explosion of cleaning chemicals and nearly lost his sight. While recovering from his accident, Wade underwent an intense spiritual conversion. Marion Wade and Ken Hansen incorporated the business in 1947, in 1958 it became ServiceMaster. The name they chose "struck us as perfect in every area. Masters of service, serving the Master," Wade explained in his autobiography, *The Lord Is My Counsel.*

As Wade integrated his belief system into his business, he viewed each individual employee and customer as someone who was made in God's image, therefore worthy of dignity and respect. His successors, Ken Hansen and Ken Wessner, also shared this strong commitment to their faith. These three leaders shaped what became the company's initial philosophy.

- To honor God in all we do.
- To help people develop.
- To pursue excellence.
- To grow profitably.

The company believed that developing every employee to his or her full potential would result in a greater quality of service. For that reason, training at all levels became ServiceMaster's fundamental strategy. The company established one of the United States' first franchise businesses. Today, the company brands include TruGreen, ChemLawn, Terminix, American Home Shield, Furniture Medic, AmeriSpec, ServiceMaster Clean, InStar Services Group, and Merry Maids.

In the 1980s, Chairman and former Chief Executive Officer C. William Pollard led the company's remarkable growth and prosperity. Pollard's book, *The Soul of the Firm*, details their philosophy and success.

The ServiceMaster philosophy is now expressed in this way:

Honor God in All We Do

- Do the right thing.
- Treat each person with dignity and respect.
- Respect each person's spirituality.
- Protect and maintain our world.

Excel with Customers

- Serve others as we would be served.
- Make it easy for the customer.
- Stand behind our work.

Help People Develop

- Help people to do their best every day.
- Build proud, dynamic teams.
- Help people reach their goals.

Grow Profitably

- Act as good stewards of our investors' capital.
- Constantly improve and innovate.
- Meet our commitments.

Here's the fundamental principle when choosing to express your mission, values, philosophy, core beliefs, and so forth, in spiritual terms: Walk the talk. Live it. To do otherwise would be hypocritical.

The following is another story that illustrates the integration of faith and business.

Checkdate Solutions—The Guiding Principle

Drew and Sarah Hiss started an outsourced payroll service business in their basement in 1994. Twelve years later, in 2006, Checkdate Solutions and their 55 employees merged with Paycor, Inc.—now the largest privately held and fourth-largest payroll company in the United States. The couple started the business to achieve economic freedom apart from what Drew calls the traditional career track of corporate America. He wanted the freedom to grow a business while simultaneously utilizing his own creativity.

Drew's early career experience included a multilevel network marketing venture and brief stints with three different companies, where he learned some valuable lessons about what to do and what not to do. At the outset, Drew had a little bit of cash, an SBA loan, and another small loan from his supportive grandmother. Checkdate's competition was formidable—large, well-known payroll companies, ADP and Paychex. Initially, the company was called Paydata, and the first several years were challenging. But Drew and Sarah pressed into their faith and persevered through character-building struggles that nearly forced them to close the doors.

Over the next 10 years, Drew was able to carve out a specialized niche by serving small and mid-size organizations. These clients value the company's flexible technology and responsive, competent service. Though the business was high-tech, it was even more "high-touch."

In 2004, Drew utilized the process described in this book to reinvigorate the business and stimulate new energy and engagement. The leaders and associates became more involved in planning, achieving, and celebrating their forward progress. The team took on new technology, moved to a new location, and rebranded the company to set it apart from the competition. New identity Checkdate Solutions now had more energy and enthusiasm about its future. Service levels improved, customer loyalty metrics were at all-time highs, and the company opened a new office in St. Louis.

Redefining the company's vision, mission, and values got them out of what Drew called "camping mode" and back on the track for growth. In the early days, the company's values were lived but unwritten. Drew and Sarah were hard-working, fun-loving, and operated with absolute integrity. They identified new values during the planning process—including honesty, integrity, humility, and respect. Eventually, all the owners committed to a higher standard, and the company's guiding principle became: "To honor God in all we do." Sound familiar? Other key leaders and teammates also committed to this new standard. Drew said that this higher (pun intended) standard became a point of accountability for all members of the team.

The owners were committed to ensure that the vision, mission, values, and guiding principle were a living, breathing part of the culture and not merely an ivory tower exercise that created a meaningless plaque in Checkdate's reception area. The mission of the company was to "Help clients save time, reduce stress, and enjoy payroll."

Checkdate Solutions was one of only three companies consecutively recognized on the Corporate List of 100 Fastest Growing Kansas City Companies for a nine-year period from 1997 to 2006.

As you create vision, mission, and values for your organization, you will want to integrate your highest aspirations. Businesses as diverse as Ben and Jerry's and ServiceMaster have earned the respect of the public and achieved extraordinary results by walking their talk.

CHAPTER

Values

What Standards Will Help Your Team Enjoy Working Together? (6 minutes)

Who you are, what your values are, what you stand for . . . They are your anchor, your north star. You won't find them in a book. You'll find them in your soul.
—Anne Mulcahy, Chairman and CEO, Xerox

I look for three things in hiring people. The first is personal integrity, the second is intelligence, and the third is a high energy level. But, if you don't have the first, the other two will kill you.
—Warren Buffett, CEO, Berkshire Hathaway

Values define your standards of behavior, your code of conduct, how people want to treat each other. Values help your team enjoy working together. They are commitments regarding how your team will treat others.

The values displayed by your senior leaders are especially important in developing your organization and its culture.

Table 5.1   Sandestin's Long-Term Aspirations

Vision	To be the Southeast's premier resort destination.
Mission	To create memories for our guests and colleagues—again and again.
Values	**A dedicated team serving with integrity, excellence, accountability, and the Golden Rule.**

Values Drive Performance and Results

As the general manager of Sandestin Golf & Beach Resort, Mike Stange had the daunting task of getting 1,400 associates on the same page. Mike first aligned his executive team, then the managers, then two different groups of 700 associates each. The outcome was a vision, mission, and values that are clear and compelling. See Table 5.1.

Printed on a small wallet-size plastic card, Mike and his team consistently use these long-term aspirations when hiring, training, and developing their associates.

In 2004 and 2005, Sandestin's region was hit with numerous hurricanes. Mike explains, "Our team really came together, and we were able to prosper during the adversity. During the tough times, our vision, mission, and values became a rally cry."

The result? Sandestin maintained its high-trust, high-performing culture and achieved its financial objectives in the midst of this challenging season—which is powerful testimony to the strength of having clear values, mission, and vision.

Why Define Your Values?

Values and behavior create your corporate culture.

Values provide:

- The standard of behavior that will help your team enjoy working together.
- Guidelines to prevent and resolve interpersonal issues.
- The foundation for a high-trust, high-performing culture.

- A foundation for strengthening relationships both inside and outside the organization.

Examples of How to Write and Display Values

Here are a few ways to effectively communicate your values.

CruiseShipCenters International:

INTEGRITY—Be open and honest while creating win-win relationships.

RESPECT—Treat others as you would like to be treated.

TEAMWORK—Provide an environment maximizing individual development.

DEDICATION—Recognize and reward those who produce results.

FUN—Love what you do and do what you love.

Z3 Graphix

Dedicated to:

- Being honest and respectful.
- Keeping a positive attitude.
- Treating others fairly.

J. Schmid:

Focused, friendly, fun, and fair

Southwest Airlines:

We are committed to providing our employees a stable work environment with equal opportunity for learning and personal growth. Creativity and innovation are encouraged for improving the effectiveness of Southwest Airlines. Above all, employees will be provided the same concern, respect, and caring attitude within the organization that they are expected to share externally with every Southwest Customer.

Real Media:

A creative, dedicated team, serving with integrity, passion, and respect.

Honeywell:

INTEGRITY and the highest ethical standards

MUTUAL RESPECT and trust in our working relationships

INNOVATION and encouragement to challenge the status quo

COMMUNICATION that is open, consistent, and two-way

TEAMWORK and meeting our commitments to one another

CONTINUOUS IMPROVEMENT, development, and learning in all we do

DIVERSITY of people, cultures, and ideas

PERFORMANCE with recognition for results

Exercise 1:3 Write Your Own Values

Place a check mark next to three to seven of the following descriptors that define the way you want your team members to treat others. Then transfer your values, in order of importance, to your business growth plan.

See Table 5.2.

Table 5.2 Examples of Values with Definitions

✅	Values
	Accountability—A personal willingness to answer for the results of my behavior
	Commitment—To maintain superior standards of quality and achievement
	Compassion—A feeling of sympathy and a strong desire to eliminate pain
	Creativity—To produce original ideas and thoughts, to bring into existence something new
	Discipline—To receive instruction and correction in a positive way: to adhere to the rules and guidelines
	Empowerment—To take personal action to achieve an agreed upon result; to give and receive power and authority
	Excellence—To engage my best efforts for the success of the organization
	Fairness—To be free from bias and injustice, to seek out other people's perspectives
	Friendly—To be favorably disposed, kind, and helpful
	Fun—To foster an environment of playfulness and enjoyment; to maintain a sense of humor
	Generosity—To give freely of my time, talent, and treasure

(continued)

(*continued*)

✓	Values
	The Golden Rule—To treat others the way I want to be treated
	Gratitude—To express thankfulness and appreciation
	Honesty—To tell the truth, to be frank and sincere in all situations
	Humility—To maintain a modest opinion of my rank or importance
	Integrity—To do what I say I will do, to adhere to ethical principles
	Life/Work Balance—To allow life to intrude on work as work intrudes on life
	Loyalty—To use difficult situations as an opportunity to demonstrate faithfulness to commitments and obligations
	Passion—To demonstrate a strong fondness and enthusiasm for the work I do
	Positive Attitude—A hopeful and constructive mind-set, feeling, and manner with regard to people and circumstances
	Respect—To esteem the worth, qualities, and abilities of another person
	Responsibility—To know and do what is expected of me
	Service—To fulfill a person's needs and expectations; to be responsive, flexible, and adaptable to his or her requirements
	Teamwork—To work together in our development, problem solving, and achievement to accomplish a shared purpose

Congratulations!

You have completed 30 percent of your business planning process. If you would like to go deeper on your Values, continue reading. To take the shortcut, go to Chapter 6.

Case Study: Jack Stack Values—Defining the Standards that Help Our Team Enjoy Working Together

JOE: How did you define your values?

CASE: It was pretty easy for us, because we had several values in our old mission statement that we wanted to revisit. We went through this exercise and we talked about our values as a team.

JOE: So you wanted to update your values?

CASE: I really wanted to just blow up the box and open up my mind to renewing everything, and approach it by acting like we didn't know anything. We wanted to go back through the entire process from the beginning, and really open ourselves up to changing our vision, mission, and values. We had established what we called our "core values," which were a part of our mission statement. These were honesty/integrity, sincerity, teamwork, and exceeding expectations.

JOE: How have these original values served you over the years?

CASE: I think very well. One of the reasons we've been successful as a restaurant in our city is because we are different. We separate ourselves through our values. There is a big gap and a lack of both honesty and integrity in many industries; especially in our own, where issues like immorality have been prevalent through the years. The fact is that we held honesty and integrity—which provide a solid moral foundation—to a high level of importance in our company. We didn't just write it down; we worked really hard to actually *live it*. I think that gave us some separation between other groups against whom we compete.

JOE: What areas of misconduct are not tolerated in your company?

CASE: For us, immoral behavior on the job includes any kind of theft or dishonesty. Beyond that, it includes actions like failing to keep promises, or not doing what you say you are going to do. Telling somebody one thing and doing another. This is another widespread issue in our industry; it's so common for people to lead others astray and tell people they're going to do something that never materializes.

JOE: So you do what you say you're going to do. How does that separate you from the competition?

CASE: In the 1980s and '90s, the restaurant industry was expanding at a rapid rate. People were opening up restaurants right and left, especially the national chains. They were building places about as fast as you can imagine. It's become so common in our industry for restaurateurs to overpromise and underdeliver. They say, "We're going to open this many stores in this much time, and you're going to be a regional manager here by this date. And there'll be this kind of bonus for you, and this is what's there for you if you join our team." I can't tell you how many people I've interviewed through the years that come in after hearing something like that.

So I admit to them that I'm not going to make those kinds of promises. I tell them that this is who we are, this is where we are today, and this is where I think they would fit in our organization. I know it doesn't sound quite as good as what you've been used to hearing, but the difference is it will *really* happen this way. It's not enough for some people; they'd rather have the promise. But I've never felt comfortable encouraging people to believe something that I'm really not confident about or ready to commit to.

JOE: What impact does it have on people when promises are made and not kept, or when management lacks integrity?

CASE: First and foremost is lost trust. They no longer are able to believe what people are telling them. This skepticism affects their ability to pour their heart into their work.

My wife, Jennifer, and I were watching the CBS show *Undercover Boss* last night. A female employee from the company being featured made the statement: "The pay comes later." Her "Undercover Boss" had been talking to her about all the work she was doing, all the different responsibilities she was picking up, and all the things that she was working on to be successful. She had just thrown herself completely into it, as if to say, "Whatever it takes, I'm going to do it." She was doing accounting, washing the windows, and cleaning out the tanks. *That's* what I'm talking about. People today want to know success before they ever start. A substantial part of maintaining honesty and integrity is letting people know that life really isn't that way. And I'm not going to make that promise to you, because I want you to understand that there's a level of commitment you have to make for your success.

JOE: In other words—you're not going to make promises to people about a get rich scheme, because it's really not the way life works.

CASE: It really comes down to bringing somebody in expecting them to work hard and using the opportunity we provide to exceed their own expectations.

JOE: What are your new values and what do they mean to you and your team?

CASE: *Integrity* means doing what you say you're going to do. *Respect* means treating one another—and ourselves—well. You have to be able to respect yourself in order to be able to respect others. *Passion* is just enjoying doing what we do. It is a genuine enjoyment and joy of life and what we're here to accomplish. *Positive Attitude* is the one thing you get to choose when you wake up every morning; so, you might as well choose the right one. Everything is more fun if you can see the good in it. *Excellence* relates to how high we want to set the bar. We have absolutely no desire to ever be average at anything we do, and we'll never consider average to be acceptable. We are always going to strive to be our best and to be excellent at what we do. *Teamwork* is based on the truth that "Two are better than one." The more our team gives to each other, the more they receive from the team. *Service* means treating our guests as family. If my family comes to my house for a meal, I want them to have a great experience. So, I have a healthy nervousness. When we serve our customers, we have a healthy edge. It's game day. It's show time. It's why we come to work.

Here is the vision, mission, and values of Jack Stack Barbecue. See Table 5.3.

Table 5.3 Jack Stack Barbecue's Long-Term Aspirations

Vision	The Nation's Premier Provider of Kansas City Barbecue
Mission	Creating Remarkable Barbecue Experiences
Values	Integrity, Respect, Passion, Positive Attitude, Excellence, Teamwork, and Service

Values Come to Life through the Stories We Tell

Leaders teach and masterful teachers illustrate their meaning with memorable stories. Storytellers reinforce cultural values through the stories they tell about all kinds of people from Mother Teresa to Abraham Lincoln to Ghandi, and the person next door.

To reinforce your organization's values:

1. Catch people doing something right and
2. Tell their stories.

Here are some stories that illustrate each of the values. Notice how the values come to life through stories—positive or negative.

The Value of Accountability—Put a Dollar in the "I CAN"

In one of my first sales jobs, the business owner had a unique way of teaching accountability. Anytime someone violated the company's code of conduct, they were required to put a dollar in the "I CAN." The leader's philosophy was simple. He said, "I can. You can. Anybody can, if you eliminate the excuses."

This leader would simply not tolerate excuses. He would say, "Excuses are just a way to fail with honor. Eliminate the excuses and you eliminate the failure." I can still hear those words 30 years later.

For example, show up late for a meeting—put a dollar in the "I CAN." Make an excuse for why you're late and put another dollar in the "I CAN." I ended up putting a lot of money in the "I CAN." It was an interesting way to hold one another accountable. The price of being "called out" by a co-worker was only a dollar, but it allowed the company to create an environment of accountability, positive attitude, teamwork, respect, and excellence.

The Value of Commitment—Toyota's Reputation

How quickly a stellar reputation can be damaged. After years of glowing recommendations from many car buffs, Toyota suddenly faced a brutal assault.

The massive Toyota recall announcement in 2010 came too late for many reporters' tastes. Toyota's delayed response to this problem—and the quality concerns that come with the recalls—damaged their reputation significantly and brought their commitment to quality into question.

Whether Toyota revives its good name is yet to be seen, but it's an excellent reminder of how quickly a reputation can be tarnished.

If you want to have a good reputation in business, you *must* be committed to superior standards of quality and achievement. Don't let your guard down. Commitment is ongoing; it's not a onetime event.

The Value of Compassion–Real Life at Silver Dollar City

Joel Manby, CEO of Herschend Family Entertainment, went undercover to learn more about his organization, while the TV show *Undercover Boss* captured his lessons learned.

What he discovered was real life.

Joel encountered single moms struggling to afford day care, a man who lost his home due to fire, and a previously homeless single mom. Compassion welled up inside of him as he got to know each of these employees and their struggles on a personal level.

Out of that compassion flowed generosity and true concern for those who had served Silver Dollar City faithfully. Due to Manby's experience on the show, his company now has new policies and practices that display greater compassion for its employees. Manby wanted to eliminate his valued team members' pains and sufferings to the best of his ability. His compassion, however, did not come until he was able to better understand their plight.

Do you know those around *you* well enough to know who needs compassion?

The Value of Creativity–Developing the Talent that Surrounds You

In the same episode of *Undercover Boss*, Manby has a humorous exchange with a young employee who tells him that he dreams of being the CEO of Silver Dollar City. This ambitious employee didn't know he was talking to the current CEO, he thought Manby was a frontline employee. This ambitious young man revealed his God-given talent and creativity when he pulled out a detailed rendering of a roller coaster ride he had designed.

The fact that this young man was a customer service manager instead of an engineer made his creativity even more remarkable. At the end of *Undercover Boss* Manby rewards and recognizes this young man's talent with a college scholarship—a chance to further develop his talents. Silver Dollar City also agreed to pay him full-time wages while he attends school.

Wise leaders like Joel Manby identify the creative talents of others, develop those talents, and use people's creativity to bring value to others.

Do you know the kinds of gifts that your employees possess? How might you discover them?

The Value of Discipline–Fruitful Discipline

In late 2009, countless people watched to see how Bernie Madoff—the man who ran the biggest investment fraud in history—would be made to pay for his crimes. After significant work, the Securities Exchange Commission (SEC) finally resolved the civil fraud charges against him. Unfortunately, the SEC settled with Madoff *without* requiring him to admit wrongdoing. Although this is not uncommon for the SEC, it is somewhat curious considering Madoff's previous admission of guilt.

Discipline requires that people follow the rules and guidelines. When people fall short, the purpose of discipline is to educate, instruct, correct, or punish. Effective discipline should restore all parties as best as possible. This includes justice for those who have been wronged and doing what's necessary to correct the offender's behavior in the future.

As we discipline ourselves and others, we adhere to the rules and guidelines. When we fall short, there is an opportunity to learn from our mistakes and make things right.

The Value of Empowerment–*The Life of Manny!*
or Sharing the Glory

The Life of Manny is an intriguing book on leadership that follows a character named Manny as he accepts a management position in a large consulting practice in New York. His first challenge comes in the form of Linda, a member of his staff who had counted on getting Manny's position. While Linda attempts to find ways to undermine her new boss, Manny tries his best to empower her. He surprisingly passes on his own opportunity for glory to Linda during one particular instance. Rather than making a presentation to a new prospect with his boss in attendance, Manny gives Linda the privilege of doing so. His selfless act results in a new client *and* a new ally.

Empowerment gives authority away to others in order for a bigger purpose to be accomplished. It takes a confident leader to empower others.

The Value of Excellence–And Beyond

An April 3, 2010, *Wall Street Journal* article stated that when there's an obvious superstar in a competition, the rest of the competitors will do worse than normal. Applied macroeconomist Jennifer Brown's research on golf found this to be particularly true.

Ms. Brown discovered that when Tiger Woods competed, the rest of the players played significantly worse than usual. They had a tendency to give up on obtaining first place. She also discovered this to be true in many other competitive environments, including in corporate America.

So what exactly happens here? When we compare ourselves to others, our results can be self-limiting. If we instead focus on always doing *our* very best—while serving a higher purpose rather than comparing ourselves to a superstar—we will reveal true excellence.

The Value of Fairness–Corruption in Russia

A research group in Moscow called the INDEM Foundation claims that Russians spent almost $320 billion in bribes last year. According to an April 20, 2010, *New York Times* article, this is two-and-a-half times more than the Russian government collects in annual revenue.

Corruption in Russia has skyrocketed in the last few years, making it one of the world's most corrupt nations. When societies begin to determine justice by the amount of material wealth that people have, a sense of both hope and fairness rapidly disappear. Bribes take away poor individuals' opportunities for justice and allow the wealthy access to injustice for their personal gains. This results in a broken economic system.

We need to stand firm against evil and demand justice and fairness. Without it many will be treated unfairly.

The Value of Being Friendly—The Security Guard with an Attitude

The last thing Rick Boxx expected at 4:30 in the morning from the security officer checking boarding passes at the airport was a warm, friendly greeting. However, Bob—the security officer—engaged in lighthearted fun with almost everyone. He was having so much fun that Rick had to ask, "Why?" Bob explained, "Even though my wife divorced me, I lost my house, and I had a massive heart attack that should have killed me, I'm blessed to be alive and thankful every day. I had a strong faith before, but now it's much stronger."

When trials come your way, you can choose to be friendly or nasty. Bob overcame his circumstances and chose to be friendly. Which approach do you think is better for you and your company? Which will *you* choose today?

The Value of Fun—Those Crazy Cows

An old proverb teaches, "A cheerful heart is good medicine, but a crushed spirit dries up the bones."

At a reception hosted by Chick-fil-A President Dan Cathy played one of their recent cow commercials. Millions of viewers have experienced a hearty laugh while watching the famous white and black cows that have trouble spelling. This particular advertisement revealed several cows parachuting into a football stadium and taking out the hamburger vendor. Not only has Chick-fil-A brought laughter to many people with their award-winning commercials, they have also managed to sell a lot of chicken.

If you have the choice between a serious business presentation and a humorous one, don't forget the value in delivering the good medicine of laughter. Bringing joy and entertainment to others enhances your mood—and may increase your bottom line as well.

The Value of Generosity–Eager to Give

The Barnhart brothers didn't want wealth to get in the way of their faith or their generosity. They decided, on starting their company Barnhart Crane and Rigging, that it would be used to fund worthwhile causes, rather than personal wealth.

Many people have those kinds of convictions in the beginning of a new venture, but most get distracted by their own needs and desires. The Barnharts, however, were different. They eventually donated 99 percent of their business to a charitable foundation, which has resulted in more than $1 million per month going to charitable causes.

During a recent interview, Alan Barnhart was asked, "When you are not working, what do you do for fun?" He said, "I have six kids and most of my non-working time revolves around them. I am a Boy Scout leader and love camping and hiking. My wife, Katherine and I are active in our church and have a passion for helping others around the world."

We make a living by what we get. We make a life by what we give.

The Value of the Golden Rule–A Judge and a Hero

According to an April 2008 *Washington Post* story, a newly married deaf couple named Deborah Morris and Louis Swann were about to be evicted over $250 in back rent. They were unable to pay their rent because of a significant cut in their disability benefits, due to their recent marriage.

Then, in stepped their unlikely hero, Judge McDonough. As the judge listened to their case, something compelled him to action. He abruptly left the courtroom, returning with $250 of his own cash. "Consider it paid," he reportedly said to the landlord's attorney.

This act of kindness resulted in an outbreak of contagious generosity. Four attorneys whipped out their checkbooks and wrote checks totaling $1,250 to further assist the couple.

Judge McDonough modeled the Golden Rule through this one selfless act: "Do unto others as you would have them do unto you,"

The Value of Gratitude—How to Elevate the Human Spirit

Many years ago I visited a popular theme park with my family. I was impressed to see the organization's vision, mission, and values prominently displayed as we walked in the park's entrance.

There was also a picture recognizing the employee of the month Denise—and shortly after we entered the park, I saw Denise in person. I approached her and congratulated her on being selected employee of the month. "This must be a great place to work," I said.

"Not really," she replied.

Surprised, I asked, "Why not?"

She responded, "People complain too much."

"Complain about what?" I wanted to know.

"First, after trying so hard to get a job here, they complain about the work; second, they complain about the weather—why complain about something you can't change? And third, they complain about the customers—as if to say this wouldn't be such a bad place to work if it weren't for all those customers bothering us all the time."

It's one thing to have a set of values displayed for people to see; it's another thing to *live* those values on a daily basis. These are the elements that create your company's culture, and which, in large part, determine the quality of your job satisfaction.

Thanksgiving and gratitude elevate the human spirit, while complaining kills the spirit. We have a choice each day to complain or display an attitude of gratitude. Clearly, one of these options makes for a much more profitable and enjoyable business.

The Value of Honesty—Dog Food Deception

More than $100,000 of merchandise was stolen from a Target store in Kansas City. Two employees worked together to steal the various products, including dog food. According to the March 17, 2010, *Kansas City*

Star article, the employees began donating stolen supplies to a dog sanctuary; however, their theft eventually turned into a profitable enterprise. By marking items as "defective," they were able to remove inventory without being caught—that is, until another employee witnessed their crime.

Though we can't guarantee that people will always be honest, we can work to protect our businesses by modeling and encouraging honesty. This is best done by displaying it through our own behavior. Showing employees that the business is honest in all of its dealings will establish a standard for all to follow.

Honesty is the best policy. It builds trust with employees and customers.

The Value of Humility–Executive Retention

Chances are that you—like most employers—would like to retain your best employees. According to an October 26, 2009, *Wall Street Journal* article titled, "How to Keep Your Best Executives," the ideal way to do that is to serve *their* needs more than your own.

According to the article, companies that help their executives be more valuable to others effectively retain their best workers for longer. By listening to employee needs and meeting those needs loyalty is encouraged.

Serving others requires humility, an ingredient missing in many workplaces. If you are a leader who desires to keep your best talent, remember to set aside your own self-interest and try a little humility from time to time. It will go a long way in keeping the best people around for years to come.

The Value of Integrity–It's Always Worth the Price

There's a story of a CEO and his team who reportedly flew to Russia in a corporate jet to discuss doing business overseas. While they were there, they discovered that their jet wasn't safe to return in unless they replaced a part. However, they learned that obtaining the part would require that they offer a bribe to the company providing their travel.

Amazingly, the CEO refused to give in to the bribe. He stayed in Russia longer than planned, eventually taking a commercial flight home. The pilots stayed until another source for the part was found.

The time of these busy executives was worth more than the amount of the bribe, yet they stood firm against corruption. Integrity is at times costly, but it doesn't make it any less right.

How much are you willing to endure and sacrifice to do the right thing?

The Value of Life/Work Balance–Enjoy a Day of Rest

Only 40 percent of the workforce today—compared to 51 percent in 1999—is "very satisfied" with their ability to balance their work and family life, according to a 2010 John J. Heldrich Center for Workforce Development's study. Why are so many people struggling with life/work balance?

The Internet has had a tremendous impact on our work over the past decade. With information flowing 24/7, and in larger volume, it's increased the demands on staff. Many people now regularly work seven days a week—whether they're technically "in" the office or not—rather than a more normal five or six.

There was a time when working on Sunday was not even *permitted* in most of our nation's industries. This was to allow people the ability to attend their place of worship and give them physical and mental rest.

If you desire better balance in your life, consider saving one day a week for solemn rest, and encouraging your employees to do the same. No one can keep going full-speed all the time; you need a break, no matter how short, to regroup and recharge.

The Value of Loyalty–Loyal Employers Are Hard to Find

Profits or people? Choosing one over the other is a common dilemma for business leaders; but rarely is it quite as dramatic a choice as it was after September 11, 2001. The airline industry has typically been financially unstable, but in one day, they fell completely into the abyss.

Airline managements' reactions to this sudden crisis revealed something about the character of each business, and the way that one carrier in particular—Southwest Airlines—handled this blow was especially insightful.

While countless other airlines immediately began slashing jobs by the thousands, Southwest became the industry maverick. Their silence when it came to announcing layoffs spoke volumes. Their loyalty to their staff has been a contrast to many others in their industry, and this tendency was highlighted in this time of intense turmoil.

Take a cue from Southwest and don't automatically assume that slashing jobs is the only answer during challenging economic times. You may discover that over the long term—as Southwest has—that your loyalty will beget loyalty from your people in return.

The Value of Passion–A Value at Any Price

A colleague of mine and his family recently spent a night at a Motel 6 in Illinois. The following night, they stayed at the Renaissance PineIsle Resort in Lake Lanier Islands, Georgia. The first night they desired an inexpensive clean room. The next night they expected service, entertainment, and pleasant surroundings.

Both businesses provided lodging, but each had a distinctly different approach. Neither approach is wrong—as long as they both perform with passion.

Motel 6's passion is providing a clean and inexpensive room. The Renaissance's, however, is to provide entertainment and service, in addition to a very nice room.

If you work passionately, it won't matter whether you serve people the basics for an inexpensive price, or you provide them with lavish surroundings and service for a higher price. If done with passion, you will shine.

Are you passionate about your work? Do you perform services and/ or provide products to the best of your ability—to a degree that will make your customers take notice?

The Value of Positive Attitude–Attitude Makes a Difference

Business leaders have options in the midst of economic turmoil. They can either choose to participate in the recession, pulling back their growth efforts and downsizing. Or, they can view it as an opportunity.

Their future may improve or deteriorate depending on their attitude and approach. The business leaders who seem to weather storms the best are the ones who have set aside worry, and have instead seized the opportunity to go after new business with a positive attitude.

Though many circumstances cannot be changed, our attitude isn't one of these. If it's been difficult for you to establish a sense of peace at work lately, stop and consider the power of a positive attitude. It can bring you peace, and put you on the road to prosperity.

Do you view your problems as opportunities? Do you have a positive attitude?

The Value of Respect—Values Can Be Learned

My wife, Diane, has incredible people skills. Since our wedding on December 17, 1983, I've never seen her be rude to another person. I, on the other hand, am not nearly as nice a person as my wife. In fact, hanging around my wife for the past quarter century has been good for my reputation. Somehow people think more of me because I would associate with a person of her caliber. I'm becoming a better person, too, because of Diane's influence.

Here are some lessons I'm learning from my wife:

- Always smile at the people you meet.
- Be exceptionally courteous.
- Say and do things that make other people feel good.
- Be quick to laugh and make other people laugh.
- Go out of your way to include people that might feel left out.
- Be a good listener.
- Don't be in such a big hurry. Smell the roses. Enjoy other people—and they'll enjoy you.

The Value of Responsibility—An Expensive High

Olympian Michael Phelps had an expensive evening when he was captured on a cell phone camera smoking pot. Former sponsor and cereal company Kellogg's decided that Phelps' behavior was not in line with their image, and refused to renew his $1 million contract. Although the majority of companies that have paid for Mr. Phelps' endorsement have chosen to continue their relationship, Kellogg's serves children and takes their responsibility to their customers seriously.

This situation reminds us that poor behavior *does* come at a cost. What is done in private can easily wind up on the front page of the newspaper—or anywhere on the Internet. Many people would like to believe that what they do on their own time doesn't matter to their business—but it does. If you want to be safe, always behave responsibly—and as if someone is watching.

The Value Service–A Boy Scout Tradition

My friend, Rick Boxx, recently attended an awards ceremony where a young man received his Eagle Scout designation from the Boy Scouts. One of the special assignments required to become an Eagle is to design, develop, and perform a community service project. The story made me think of my older brother, Mike, also an Eagle Scout, and someone who still serves with excellence in his business and in his relationships.

The Boy Scouts wisely understand that young men need to serve others well, including their community. Although many people assume that leadership is about power and selfish interests, the Boy Scouts train young men to serve. Most of the young men who have this foundation from which to grow inevitably end up doing their communities, companies, and families a world of good in coming years.

If you study great leaders, you will discover people who have humbly served others, rather than touting their own greatness. As you work in the marketplace, don't forget the importance of serving others. The Boy Scout oath emphasizes the importance of "helping others at all times"—and isn't that the purpose of many extraordinary businesses?

The Value of Teamwork–Moments of Truth

When Jan Carlson became CEO of Scandinavian Airlines, the company was rated as the worst airline in the world. The company was rated last in service, dependability, and profits as a percentage of sales. One year later, they were ranked number one in all three categories. The turn-around is a tribute to the power of teamwork.

Carlson encouraged his 20,000 employees to make every customer contact as pleasant and as memorable as possible. The company had about 10 million customers each year and Carlson figured that each customer made contact with about five of his people for very short, yet critical periods of time. Carlson called these 50 million brief customer interactions "moments of truth." Pilots, flight attendants, ticket agents, baggage handlers, and other airline employees realized they all had a part to play in the team's success. The difference between first place and last place was how well each team member performed in those moments of truth.

How about you and your team? What are your moments of truth? Is your team making every interaction pleasant and memorable?

CHAPTER

Objectives

How Will You Measure Success? (7 minutes)

Too often we measure everything and understand nothing. The three most important things you need to measure in a business are customer satisfaction, employee satisfaction, and cash flow.
—Jack Welch, Former Chairman and CEO, General Electric

Picking the right numbers to track for your business is one of the most important decisions you can make. People do what gets measured.
—Michael LeBoeuf, PhD, Author and Consultant

Management by objectives works if you first think through your objectives. 90% of the time you haven't.
—Peter Drucker, Father of Modern Management

Objectives are measures of your success and organizational performance.

Growth-focused objectives include customer measures, employee measures, and financial measures.

Greed Is (Not) Good!

For many, the purpose of business is deeply misunderstood. Think about the character Gordon Gekko in the movie *Wall Street*, who said, "Greed, for lack of a better word, is good. Greed is right. Greed works. Greed clarifies. Cuts through and captures the essence of the evolutionary spirit. Greed, in all of its forms—has marked the upward surge of mankind." Gordon's immoral thinking led to his dishonest actions and lousy results. Like Bernie Madoff, he ended up in jail.

Years ago, I asked Lee Wagy, an extraordinary McDonald's franchisee how he helped his teenage workers become such outstanding employees. He explained, "I teach them enlightened self-interest. The better they serve others—customers, co-workers, and owners—the better they serve themselves in terms of career advancement, financial rewards, recognition, and job security." This is how wealth is produced and real success is achieved: countless individuals seek to meet their own needs by meeting the needs of others.

Research funded by Harvard Business School found that companies that "obsessively" focused on meeting customers', employees', and owners' needs—while developing leadership at all levels—outperformed comparison companies in four critical areas:

1. Revenues increase 4 times faster.
2. Job creation is 7 times greater.
3. Owner equity grows 12 times faster.
4. Profit performance is 756 times higher.

It's not really rocket science, is it? Growing an extraordinary business may be a lot of hard work, but it's really not complicated at its core. The purpose of a business is to serve customers, employees, and owners while developing leaders.

Your One Hour Plan for Growth will serve you best if you serve others and keep track of your progress.

Why Set Objectives?

The game of business is more productive, rewarding, and fun when you keep score.

Objectives provide:

- A balanced set of measures that will help you take your business to the next level.
- Targets to aim for, because measures stimulate higher achievement.
- Something to celebrate.

How to Write Objectives

Follow these three simple steps when writing your objectives: (1) Determine *what* to measure. Keep it simple. (2) Determine *how* to measure it. This may take some time, so be patient. (3) Set your objective. This is your true measure of success.

Some examples are shown in Table 6.1.

Table 6.1 How to Write Objectives—Examples

		What to Measure	How to Measure It	Objective	✓
Customer Measures		Customer Satisfaction	Two Question Survey*	70	
		Market Share	% of business in your market area	60%	
		Customer Retention	% of customers who stay with you from year to year	95%	
		Number of Customers	# of different people or companies you serve	150	
Employee Measures		Productivity-Revenue per Employee	Revenue divided by # of employees	$150,000	
		Productivity-Profit per Employee	Profit divided by # of Employees	$15,000	
		Employee Satisfaction	Organizational Health Assessment*	3.2	
		Leadership Development	# of employees completing leadership development process	12	
Financial Measures		Gross Revenue	Annually in Dollars	$1,500,000	
		Profit	Annually in Dollars	$150,000	
		EBITDA	Annually in Dollars	$200,000	
		Debt	In Dollars	0	

*Service offered by Joe Calhoon

Exercise 1:4 Write Your Own Objectives

- **Determine what to measure.** Keep it simple; straightforward measures lead to easily understood, clear-cut business operations.
- **Determine how to measure it.** You may need to take a survey, facilitate focus groups, or hire an outside vendor to get a benchmark established. Be patient; it can take some time to establish a good system of measurements.
- **Set your objective.** This is the numerical objective. If your first employee survey measures 2.6 on a 4.0 scale, you might set an objective of 3.0.

See Table 6.2.

Table 6.2 How to Write Objectives

	What to Measure	How to Measure It	Objective
Customer Measures			
Employee Measures			
Financial Measures			

Write your top three to five objectives and transfer these to your business growth plan.

_____

_____

_____

_____

_____

Congratulations!

You have completed 42 percent of your business planning process.

If you would like to go deeper on your Objectives, continue reading.

To take the shortcut, go to Chapter 7.

Case Study: Jack Stack Barbecue— How We Measure Our Success

This interview features Travis Carpenter, a vice president with Jack Stack Barbecue. Travis's job is to help the general managers succeed.

JOE: What are Jack Stack's most important measures of success?
TRAVIS: We're achieving our vision, fulfilling our mission, and living our values by serving our customers, creating a great working environment for our employees, and delivering bottom-line results for the owners. Those are the three areas we measure.
JOE: How do you measure customer satisfaction?
TRAVIS: We have an intensive Secret Shopper program that provides us scores every month. We also measure the cleanliness and sanitation of every store through an inspection called a "Golden Pit Fork." And we receive comments every day from our customers. We share that information with our team on a regular basis.

Joe: How do you measure your employee satisfaction?

Travis: We gauge employee satisfaction by utilizing Manager's Surveys and the Organizational Health Assessment.

Joe: What about the financial measures?

Travis: Our main focus is top-line revenue. We also measure EBITDA, which stands for earnings before interest, taxes, depreciation, and amortization.

Joe: Could you describe in more detail some of your measures—specifically the customer and employee tools. How would you describe the Secret Shopper process?

Travis: We use a third-party company to send mystery shoppers to each store three times a month, so each store is evaluated by secret shoppers 36 times annually. The secret shoppers come in to experience our dining room at lunch or dinner, as well as our carry-out facilities. After the service is provided, they complete a series of questions that rate us based on that experience. Some questions are subjective, such as: would you return, would you recommend us, tell me about your overall experience. Others are very objective; they cover timing on when food was served, when the server came to the table, how often drinks were refilled, that sort of thing. It gives us a good snapshot of a guest experience.

The Secret Shopper program is pretty intensive. Shoppers give us a 12- to 15-page written report (depending on how long each section is) that covers about 130 areas. They write a narrative on each graded section of the restaurant including the dining room service, cleanliness, bar service, and so on.

We take this feedback very seriously, and appreciate the detail provided. It covers everything from the parking lot, to the decor on the walls, to hospitality—just about everything you could possibly imagine. We use those scores as part of our manager compensation program.

Joe: How often do you conduct the Health and Cleanliness Inspection?

Travis: The managers perform the inspection monthly and our director of operations, Rod Toelkes, conducts a quarterly inspection that's scored. It's a highly comprehensive process. Rod goes through each store and evaluates everything that the guest can see or touch. He rates every area of the restaurant on a scale of one to four from unacceptable to exceptional—including carpets and walls, tables and chairs, under the counters, everything from the front door to the back door. He assesses cleanliness, organization, health, and safety.

JOE: Do you have any data that measures customer retention?

TRAVIS: We use customer counts and same store sales. This is something we are working on this year, because we believe there is a definite need for additional ways to measure customer satisfaction. The other area that we are currently utilizing to evaluate customer satisfaction is the comments we receive from our raving fans, and the occasional not-so-satisfied customer. We receive these every day, and share any potential areas of improvement with anyone who can do something about the issues at hand. We share the positive comments with the entire company.

JOE: How do you go about sharing those comments with your team?

TRAVIS: John Lee, our director of training, picks a few of the comments every week and puts them in our newsletter. We post that for our entire team to read. Here are a few examples:

- A couple drove all the way from Omaha, Nebraska, to Kansas City just so that the birthday boy could have Jack Stack Barbecue. They claimed the food and atmosphere were well worth the two-and-a-half-hour drive.

- The Copper Mountain Ski Patrol was in to eat. They had been all over the country promoting the resort, and decided to end their trip in Kansas City. They had some barbecue in Lawrence, Kansas, the night before and were very disappointed; so they asked around and heard from locals that Jack Stack Barbecue was the best barbecue in the city and decided to check us out. They were blown away with the taste and said that their experience with us completely redeemed what they had been told about the true taste of Kansas City barbecue! The group inquired when a Jack Stack was going to open in Colorado—preferably at the base of Copper Mountain.

- We had some first-time guests come in from Minneapolis. They were on their way to Florida and were told they *had* to stop and have Jack Stack Barbecue. The Jack's Best was their choice and they absolutely loved it. They promised me this would be a stop for them from now on, and grabbed a catalog on the way out.

JOE: What about your employee satisfaction measures?

TRAVIS: We all know that managers are vital in maintaining the Jack Stack culture and employee satisfaction. Twice a year, in February and August, we ask our employees to complete a survey that evaluates our organization overall and the managers. In February, employees complete an Organizational Health Assessment (OHA), and in August they complete a Manager Survey. Employees will rate every manager in the building. The feedback we gather from these, helps our managers improve in their roles.

The Organizational Health Assessment is more comprehensive. That survey evaluates how our employees are doing personally, along with their relationships with co-workers, managers, and leadership. The OHA also measures the efficiency of our systems.

JOE: How many managers are in your restaurants?

TRAVIS: There are six in the Plaza store, and there are typically either six or seven managers in a store. We have the service manager and a bar manager in the front, as well as a host/bus manager. They run the front of the building along with the general manager. We then typically have a kitchen manager with two assistant kitchen managers.

JOE: You mentioned that managers are compensated based on these customer measures. How does that work?

TRAVIS: All of the managers I just mentioned earn a percentage of the net profit, which comes in the form of a quarterly bonus. That bonus is impacted if the store does not hit their Secret Shopper Survey score, the Pit Fork score, the Manager Survey score, or the Organizational Health Assessment score. We find that what gets rewarded gets done.

JOE: It sounds like one of your business philosophies relates to sharing the wealth with those who produce results. That reminds me of a quote from Winston Churchill. He said, "The problem with socialism is that so many people share in its misery: the problem with capitalism is that so few people share in its rewards."

TRAVIS: We believe that every employee should have an opportunity to share in our success.

JOE: How do you teach business literacy to your employees? What impact does that have on financial performance?

TRAVIS: We hire lots of young people who have limited experience with business and financial matters. We have found that the more our employees learn about our business and finances, the better decisions they make, and the more conscientious they become in the work they do. Unfortunately, I know quite a few restaurant owners who don't even share their financials with their *managers*, let alone their employees. We use "The Jack Stack Dollar" during orientation and ongoing training to help people get the big picture of what it takes for our business to survive and prosper.

JOE: What's your focus when you teach people about "The Jack Stack Dollar"?

TRAVIS: We rarely talk about profits to our team members. The focus is always on top-line sales. We want to do everything we can to take care of our customers and keep them coming back for more. It's a lot easier to run a busy restaurant than a slow restaurant. But we do share information like "The Jack Stack Dollar," because we have responsibility to run a sustainable business.

JOE: Let's talk about "The Jack Stack Dollar" in greater detail (see Figure 6.1).

TRAVIS: We basically explain to our employees everything that's in each of these categories. They come to realize that a percent here and a percent there really add up, and that they can actually do something about it. Here's the breakdown:

- Food Cost includes all food and drinks.
- Labor and Benefit Cost includes salary, benefits, bonuses, taxes, and the cost of hiring people.
- Uniform and Supply Cost includes china and silverware, glasses and carry-out containers, tablecloth and napkins, and all the other supplies it takes to run our stores.
- Repairs include upgrading buildings and equipment.
- Utilities include gas, water, and electric.
- Management Fee includes leadership team and all the administrative functions in the company.

Orientation

THE JACK STACK DOLLAR

Food Cost	29.5 ¢	
Labor & Benefits Cost	30.0 ¢	
Uniform & Supply Cost	6.5 ¢	
Repairs	3.5 ¢	
Utilities	2.5 ¢	
Management Fee	9.0 ¢	
Administrative	6.5 ¢	
Real Estate, Depreciation, Insurance & Interest	6.5 ¢	
Net Profits	6.0 ¢	
	100.0 ¢	

Figure 6.1   "The Jack Stack Dollar"

- Administrative includes technology, marketing, credit card fees, office supplies, and so on.
- Real Estate, Depreciation, Insurance, and Interest are self-explanatory.
- Net Profits provide a return for the owner's investment in the business.

JOE: Is there anything else you'd like to share about objectives?

CASE: Objectives should be measureable and well defined. Incentives need to be designed to support the vision, mission, and values of your business. You can't say that one behavior is the most important, and then reward another kind of behavior; you have to maintain consistency with your employees.

Financial Literacy 101

If you are not financially independent by the time you are forty or fifty, it doesn't mean that you are living in the wrong country or at the wrong time. It simply means that you have the wrong plan.

—Jim Rohn, Business Philosopher

Three decades ago, I was struggling with major financial problems. I was in a deep financial hole. I had unsecured debt that was twice my gross annual income. A trusted advisor told me to turn my problem into a project—a wisdom project. Noah Webster defines wisdom as "the right use or exercise of knowledge." It's been a long, challenging, and rewarding project.

As Stephen Covey says, "You can't talk yourself out of a problem you behaved yourself into." Judging from the large number of businesses and people who are experiencing financial struggles, I think you'll find this brief overview to be useful. You might even want to teach these ideas to your children and grandchildren.

The two most common financial reports are the profit and loss statement and the balance sheet. Let's compare these two financial tools to your own personal finances as a way to better understand finances. The profit and loss statement is comparable to your personal income, expenses, and discretionary income. The balance sheet is comparable to what you own, what you owe, and your net worth.

The Profit and Loss Statement Made Simple

To better understand a company's profit and loss statement, let's consider your personal income and expenses. Your gross income minus payroll deductions equals your take-home pay. Your take-home pay minus your living expenses equals your discretionary income. Discretionary income is the money that you have left after paying all your living expenses. Here's an important question: Is discretionary income a good thing? (Hint: Most people don't have discretionary income. They're spending more than they make and that's where the trouble begins.) Think about it; discretionary income allows you money to pay off past debts, create a cash cushion, give to worthwhile causes, save for major purchases (like a house or a car), invest for your future, take that dream vacation, provide for your children's education, or the needs of your loved ones. Discretionary income is not a good thing . . . it's a *great* thing!

Now let's consider a company's profit and loss statement. Gross revenues minus the cost of goods sold equals gross profit. Gross profit minus overhead equals net profit. Now let me ask you: Is net profit a good thing? Profit allows organizations to build cash reserves to survive during the tough times, pay off debt, gives them the option to expand the business without borrowing, hire new employees, or provide additional

Table 6.3 The Simplified Profit and Loss Statement

Personal Finances	Business Finances
Gross Income	Gross Revenue
− Payroll Deductions	− Cost of Goods Sold
= Take-Home Pay	= Gross Profit
− Living Expenses	− Overhead
= Discretionary Income	= Net Profit

benefits for employees and owners. Profit is not a good thing . . . it's a *great* thing!

Peter Drucker wisely observed that misunderstanding the importance of profit is one of the major threats to the future of our economic system.

The Balance Sheet Made Simple

To better understand your company's balance sheet, let's think about your personal assets (what you own) minus your personal liabilities (what you owe) which equals your net worth. Personal net worth is obviously a *great* thing. Your net worth provides financial reserves and security. It can also create cash flow in the form of interest, dividends, rental income, etc.

In business, a company's balance sheet includes its assets minus its liabilities, which equal equity. When a company has a strong balance sheet, it's in a strong financial position–just like you as an individual or family.

Table 6.4 The Simplified Balance Sheet

Personal Finances	Business Finances
What You Own	Assets
− What You Owe	− Liabilities
= Net Worth	= Equity

As my mentor, Cavett Robert used to say, "Money isn't everything, but it does rank right up there with oxygen." Business profits and equity, an individual's discretionary income and net worth are the oxygen that allow us to breathe more freely, relax, and focus on serving others.

PART

Where Are You Now?

CHAPTER

Facing the Brutal Realities

What Are the Big Issues that Must Be Addressed? (10 minutes)

My job is to turn over rocks and look at the squiggly things, even if what you see can scare the hell out of you.
—Fred Purdue, Former Vice President and General Manager of Business Process, Pitney Bowes

Leadership does not begin just with vision. It begins with getting people to confront the brutal facts and to act on the implications . . . One of the primary ways to de-motivate people is to ignore the brutal facts of reality.
—Jim Collins, Author of *Good to Great*

Focus on the Few Issues that Have the Greatest Impact

In his book *Good to Great*, author Jim Collins says, "The good-to-great leaders were able to strip away so much noise and clutter and just focus on the few things that would have the greatest impact." That's what you're going to do here in the next 10 minutes.

In order to focus on the few things that have the greatest impact on your business growth, you'll want to apply the 80/20 principle.

You know the drill:

- 20 percent of your clothes are worn 80 percent of the time.
- 20 percent of the people have 80 percent of the wealth.
- 20 percent of your customers provide 80 percent of your revenue.
- 20 percent of your employees provide 80 percent of your results.
- 20 percent of your issues will lead to 80 percent of your business growth.

Of course, it's not always exactly 80/20; but the point as Richard Koch writes in his book *The 80/20 Principle*, is that, ". . . there is an inbuilt imbalance between causes and results, inputs and outputs, an effort and reward."

As you grow your business, the 80/20 principle will help you:

- Focus on what's important.
- Reduce what's not important.

There are most likely a few substantial issues in your organization that will lead to a few strategies that will make the most significant impact for your company's future. Focus on these.

To quickly identify the most critical areas to address, write the most significant issues that currently need your attention.

Exercise 2:1 What Are Your Big Issues that Need to Be Addressed in Your Organization?

Identify the five to ten major issues that must be addressed to grow your business. Please write them down on Table 7.1 and then rank them in order of importance.

Table 7.1 The Big Issues that Need to Be Addressed

Rank	Our Issues

Transfer your issues to the appropriate strategy boxes. See Table 7.2. Identify the one most important strategy to take your business to the next level. You will write that strategy in the next exercise.

(continued)

(*continued*)

Table 7.2   Write Your Issues in the Appropriate Boxes and Identify Your Most Important Strategy

Human Resources—Your people	**Innovation**—Your products and services
Physical Resources—Your equipment, resources, and physical space	**Marketing and Sales**—Selling your products and services
Financial Resources—Your access to capital	**Productivity/Delivery**—Delivering your products and services
Profit Requirements—Your ability to make a profit	**Social Responsibility**—Giving back

In Step 3, Your Issues Will Become Strategies and Priorities

Imagine your big issues relate to your people. Obviously, your most important strategy would be Human Resources. Areas of work may include hiring, training, or compensation, for example. To make progress, individuals will want to achieve specific results that address those strategic areas. The results to be accomplished are called priorities. The following table illustrates this planning process in detail. See Table 7.3.

Please review the examples on the following pages before writing your strategy in Exercise 3:1 (Chapter 8).

Table 7.3 How Issues Become Strategies and Priorities—Examples

Strategic Categories	Issues	Strategy	Priorities
Human Resources	• Untrained employees • Lack of accountability • Lack of employee engagement	**Human Resources—** Build a high-performing team through ongoing training, performance management, and increased employee engagement.	• Jill will conduct initial 2 hour training class by January 31. • Bob will conduct 8 individual employee meetings to clarify expectations by January 14. • Melinda will facilitate a team discussion regarding our new business growth plan by January 28.
Physical Resources	• Inadequate technology • Lack of proper equipment • Underutilized space	**Physical Resources—** Equip people with the tools to succeed by providing appropriate technology, equipment, and better space utilization.	• Frank will make recommendations regarding technology upgrades by January 20. • Jody will purchase new space efficient printer by January 31. • Zach will reorganize the main office to better utilize space by January 25.

(continued)

Table 7.3 *(continued)*

Strategic Categories	Issues	Strategy	Priorities
Financial Resources	• Lack of timely, accurate financial statements. • Insufficient cash reserves • Inadequate budgeting system	**Financial Resources—** Increase financial stability by hiring a new accountant, establishing a line of credit, and redesigning the budget process.	• Heather will interview 2 new accounting firms by January 21. • John will establish a $100,000 line of credit at the bank by January 28. • Kevin will redesign the budgeting system by January 17.
Innovation	• Aging product line • Less than acceptable service quality • Too few streams of income	**Innovation—** Better serve our customers by developing new products, improving our service quality, and developing multiple streams of income.	• Phil will make recommendations for 3 new products by January 24. • Bonnie will conduct a customer satisfaction survey and make specific recommendations to improve service quality by January 31. • Andrew will make recommendations on new, potential streams of income by January 10.

Table 7.3 *(continued)*

Strategic Categories	Issues	Strategy	Priorities
Marketing and Sales	• Lack of sales skills • Underutilized social media • Outdated brand	**Marketing and Sales—** Increase sales and revenues by improving sales tactics, effective utilization of social media and rebranding.	• David will sign up for 6 week sales class by January 10. • Mary will make recommendations regarding use of LinkedIn, Facebook, and Twitter by January 21. • Patrick will contract with branding vendor by January 17.
Productivity/Delivery	• Too much re-work • Ineffective hand-offs between sales and operations • Too many mistakes at our customer events.	**Productivity/Delivery—** Improve operational efficiency by improving work processes, better communication between sales and operations, and conducting post-delivery reviews.	• Sara will facilitate a half day process improvement session to minimize re-work by January 19. • Jim will facilitate a meeting between sales and operations to improve communication by January 28. • Scott will conduct post-delivery reviews after every customer event.

Table 7.3 (*continued*)

Strategic Categories	Issues	Strategy	Priorities
Profit Requirements	• Increasing costs • Inconsistent pricing structure • Lack of expense controls	**Profit Requirements—** Maximize financial performance by developing new vendor relationships, updating our pricing structure and expense controls.	• Stacy will make recommendations regarding new potential vendors by January 27. • Joe will present the new pricing structure for leadership approval by January 17. • Greg will monitor expenses on a weekly basis.
Social Responsibility	• Lack of team spirit • Not giving back to the community • Lack of involvement with worthwhile causes	**Social Responsibility—** Strengthen our community and team spirit through greater involvement in worthwhile community causes.	• Sam will organize the Habitat for Humanity service day by January 21. • Della will make recommendations regarding a new employee match program by January 31. • Amber will research worthwhile causes and post weekend volunteer sign-up sheets by January 26.

Congratulations!

You have completed 58 percent of your business planning process.

If you would like to go deeper on your Issues, turn to the Appendix.

To take the shortcut, go to Chapter 8.

PART

How Will You Get from Here to There?

CHAPTER

Strategies

What Are the Major Categories of Work to Be Done?
(15 minutes)

There is nothing as useless as doing efficiently that which should not be done at all.
— Peter Drucker, Father of Modern Management

It's very difficult to lead today when people are not really participating in the decision. You won't be able to attract and retain great people if they don't feel like they are a part of the authorship of the strategy.
— Howard Schultz, Chairman and CEO, Starbucks

Strategies are the high-level choices you make that determine the course your company is going to follow. They answer the question, "How are you going to get from where you are now to realizing your vision?" You may have as many as five strategies.

Serving the Customer Is Always a Winning Strategy

Larry Grill, former vice president of corporate services for Alabama Power, ran an eight-person leadership team that served 65 managers and supervisors, who served the 600-member corporate service staff. These 600 people serve Alabama Power's 6,000 employees, who provide electricity for more than one million residential, commercial, and industrial customers.

Larry explained his leadership philosophy: "The further you go up the corporate chart, the greater your responsibility to serve others. Unfortunately, many leaders lose the ego battle and undermine their own effectiveness. Leadership is best described as *servant leadership*."

In other words leaders serve employees, who in turn serve customers. Keep this in mind as a winning strategy for any business.

When Larry's team came together to create their plan, one of the core strategies involved developing "servant leadership." Larry Grill was an effective leader who was developing other leaders—which is another vital winning strategy.

Why Write Strategies?

Strategies may be the most important element of your business growth plan, that's why it's often called a strategic plan.

Strategies provide:

- A focus on essential areas where you work to grow your business.
- The pathways to reach your vision and fulfill your mission.
- Guidance to engage employees and better serve customers.

Exercise 3:1 Write Your Own Strategy ("Shortcut" users: Write your one most important strategy only)

1. **Name the strategy.** You already identified your most important strategy in Chapter 7. It may be human resources, physical resources, financial resources, innovation, marketing and sales, productivity/delivery, profit requirements, or social responsibility. Referring to your strategy by name ("human resources") makes it easier to communicate.

2. **Clearly define the end in mind.** What are you trying to accomplish in this area? Think about the end in mind as a mini–vision statement. Examples will be provided in each of the eight strategic areas.

3. **Use the word "by" or "through."** In other words, you are going to accomplish the end in mind "by" or "through" what follows next.

4. **Identify your strategic choices.** These are your "big picture" choices of work to be done. These strategic choices address your issues.

The following template should make the four-step process easy to understand. Once you understand how to write a strategy, turn to the strategy page that you identified in the issues section (Chapter 7) and write your one most important strategy. Then transfer that strategy to your business growth plan.

On the following page is a strategy exercise example. The next several pages are designed for you to write your one most important strategy and several others, as time allows. Table 8.1 is an example of a Human Resources Strategy Exercise.

Table 8.1 Example of the Human Resources Strategy Exercise

Strategic Category ✅		End in Mind	by/through	✅	Strategic Choices
Human Resources	√	Build a high performance team	through	√	hiring
		Expand our capacity to serve			putting the right people in the right positions
		Increase employee engagement			leadership
		Strengthen our management team		√	**training**
		Improve employee retention			management
		(write your own)			incentives
				√	**recognition**
				√	(write your own) *Cross-training*
					(write your own)

Example of Human Resources Strategy:

- Build a high performance team through effective hiring, training, recognition, and cross-training.

The next sixteen pages will help you write your most important strategies.

Note to Shortcut users: Write your one most important strategy by turning to the appropriate strategy page.

Write Your Human Resources Strategy

Instructions:

1. Place a check mark next to your "end in mind" or write your own.
2. Choose the word "by" or "through."
3. Place a check mark next to your "strategic choices" or write your own.
4. Rewrite your strategy on the next page and transfer the strategy to your business growth plan.

   See Table 8.2.

Table 8.2

Strategic Category	✓	End in Mind	by/through	✓	Strategic Choices
Human Resources		Build a high performance team			hiring
		Expand our capacity to serve			putting the right people in the right positions
		Increase employee engagement			leadership
		Strengthen our management team			training
		Improve employee retention			management
		(write your own)			incentives
					recognition
					(write your own)
					(write your own)

Write your Human Resources Strategy and transfer it to your business growth plan.

_____

_____

_____

_____

_____

Examples of Human Resources Strategies:

- Build a high-performance team through effective hiring and training.
- Build our high-trust, high-performance team through selective hiring, ongoing training, equitable compensation, and servant leadership.
- Increase employee engagement by putting the right people in the right positions and rewarding their performance.

For additional information on Human Resources Strategies, refer to Table 7.3 and the Strategic Ideas section at the end of this chapter.

Write Your Physical Resources Strategy

Instructions:

1. Place a check mark next to your "end in mind" or write your own.
2. Choose the word "by" or "through."
3. Place a check mark next to your "strategic choices" or write your own.
4. Rewrite your strategy on the next page and transfer the strategy to your business growth plan.

    See Table 8.3.

Table 8.3

Strategic Category	✓	End in Mind	by/through	✓	Strategic Choices
Physical Resources		Improve our work environment			technology
		Equip people with the tools to succeed			physical space
		Increase efficiency			equipment
		Maximize the efficiency of all our resources			space utilization
		(write your own)			energy conservation
					(write your own)
					(write your own)
					(write your own)

Write your Physical Resources Strategy and transfer it to your business growth plan.

_____

_____

_____

_____

_____

Examples of Physical Resources Strategies:

- Improve our work environment by expanding our physical space.
- Equip people with the tools to succeed by upgrading our technology and office furniture.
- Increase efficiency by utilizing appropriate technology, upgrading outdated equipment, and conserving energy.

For additional information on Physical Resources Strategies, refer to Table 7.3 and the Strategic Ideas section at the end of this chapter.

Write Your Financial Resources Strategy

Instructions:

1. Place a check mark next to your "end in mind" or write your own.
2. Choose the word "by" or "through."
3. Place a check mark next to your "strategic choices" or write your own.
4. Rewrite your strategy on the next page and transfer the strategy to your business growth plan.
   See Table 8.4.

Table 8.4

Strategic Category	✓	End in Mind	by/through	✓	Strategic Choices
Financial Resources		Obtain capital			bank financing
		Improve financial capacity			angel investors
		Increase financial stability			private equity
		Grow our business			venture capital
		(write your own)			employee ownership
					obtaining a line of credit
					(write your own)
					(write your own)
					(write your own)

Write your Financial Resources Strategy and transfer it to your business growth plan.

_____

_____

_____

_____

_____

Examples of Financial Resources Strategies:

• Increase financial stability by obtaining a line of credit.
• Enhance our capacity for growth through bank financing and employee ownership.
• Obtain capital by exploring bank financing, angel investors, and private equity.

For additional information on Financial Resources Strategies, refer to Table 7.3 and the Strategic Ideas section at the end of this chapter

Write Your Innovation Strategy

Instructions:

1. Place a check mark next to your "end in mind" or write your own.
2. Choose the word "by" or "through."
3. Place a check mark next to your "strategic choices" or write your own.
4. Rewrite your strategy on the next page and transfer the strategy to your business growth plan.
    See Table 8.5.

Table 8.5

Strategic Category	✔	End in Mind	by/through	✔	Strategic Choices
Innovation		Develop multiple streams of income			developing new products
		Develop a competitive advantage			developing new services
		Better serve our customers			improving products
		Increase business longevity			improving services
		(write your own)			(write your own)
					(write your own)
					(write your own)
					(write your own)

Write your Innovation Strategy and transfer it to your business growth plan.

_____

_____

_____

_____

_____

Examples of Innovation Strategies:

- Develop multiple streams of income by offering new products and services to our niche market.
- Develop our competitive advantage by learning best practices and experimentation.
- Create new, desirable, high-margin products through industry observation, customer interviews, and focus groups.

For additional information on Innovation Strategies, refer to Table 7.3 and the Strategic Ideas section at the end of this chapter.

Write Your Marketing and Sales Strategy

Instructions:

1. Place a check mark next to your "end in mind" or write your own.
2. Choose the word "by" or "through."
3. Place a check mark next to your "strategic choices" or write your own.
4. Rewrite your strategy on the next page and transfer the strategy to your business growth plan.
   See Table 8.6.

Table 8.6

Strategic Category	✓	End in Mind	by/through	✓	Strategic Choices
Marketing and Sales		Build our brand			determining the ideal customer
		Expand market share			understanding customer wants and needs
		Focus on our niche			database management
		Increase sales and revenues			defining marketing message
		(write your own)			marketing communication
					needs focused selling
					rebranding
					(write your own)

Write your Marketing and Sales Strategy and transfer it to your business growth plan.

_____

_____

_____

_____

_____

Examples of Marketing and Sales Strategies:

- Increase lead generation by improving our website, strengthening our online marketing efforts, and asking for referrals.
- Build our brand by developing and communicating our marketing message.
- Attract more customers through targeted direct marketing campaigns, customer workshops, and public relations.

For additional information on Marketing and Sales Strategies, refer to Table 7.3 and the Strategic Ideas section at the end of this chapter.

Write Your Productivity/Delivery Strategy

Instructions:

1. Place a check mark next to your "end in mind" or write your own.
2. Choose the word "by" or "through."
3. Place a check mark next to your "strategic choices" or write your own.
4. Rewrite your strategy on the next page and transfer the strategy to your business growth plan.
        See Table 8.7.

Table 8.7

Strategic Category	✓	End in Mind	by/through	✓	Strategic Choices
Productivity/ Delivery		Meet customer expectations			improving customer service
		Deliver quality experiences			monitoring standards of performance
		Improve operational efficiency			improving workflow systems
		Improve quality			improving process literacy
		(write your own)			conducting post-delivery reviews
					(write your own)
					(write your own)
					(write your own)

Write your Productivity/Delivery Strategy and transfer it to your business growth plan.

_____

_____

_____

_____

_____

Examples of Productivity/Delivery Strategies:

• Improve productivity through process improvement and utilization of effective technology.
• Improve customer service by improving workflow systems and conducting postdelivery reviews.
• Improve efficiency by setting and monitoring standards of performance.

For additional information on Productivity/Delivery Strategies, refer to Table 7.3 and the Strategic Ideas section at the end of this chapter.

Write Your Profit Requirements Strategy

Instructions:

1. Place a check mark next to your "end in mind" or write your own.
2. Choose the word "by" or "through."
3. Place a check mark next to your "strategic choices" or write your own.
4. Rewrite your strategy on the next page and transfer the strategy to your business growth plan.
    See Table 8.8.

Table 8.8

Strategic Category	✅	End in Mind	by/through	✅	Strategic Choices
Profit Requirements		Improve return on investment			developing a financial plan
		Maximize financial performance			hiring a CPA
		Achieve profit objectives			partnering with a banker
		Increase profits			AP/AR process
		(write your own)			teaching financial literacy
					(write your own)
					(write your own)

Write your Profit Requirements Strategy and transfer it to your business growth plan.

_____

_____

_____

_____

_____

Examples of Profit Requirements Strategies:

- Increase profits by effectively budgeting and monitoring financial performance.
- Strengthen our financial position by selling unnecessary assets.
- Improve financial performance by hiring a competent CPA, effectively managing accounts receivable, and teaching financial literacy to our team.

For additional information on Profit Requirement Strategies, refer to Table 7.3 and the Strategic Ideas section at the end of this chapter.

Write Your Social Responsibility Strategy

Instructions:

1. Place a check mark next to your "end in mind" or write your own.
2. Choose the word "by" or "through."
3. Place a check mark next to your "strategic choices" or write your own.
4. Rewrite your strategy on the next page and transfer the strategy to your business growth plan.
      See Table 8.9.

Table 8.9

Strategic Category	✔	End in Mind	by/through	✔	Strategic Choices
Social Responsibility		Give back			donating
		Strengthen our communities			partnering
		Contribute to worthwhile causes			leadership
		Care for the needy			employee involvement
		(write your own)			volunteering
					community service
					(write your own)
					(write your own)

Write your Social Responsibility Strategy and transfer it to your business growth plan.

_____

_____

_____

_____

_____

Examples of Social Responsibility Strategies:

• Give back to our community by partnering with United Way and promoting our Employee Match Program.
• Contribute to worthwhile causes by offering incentives for employee involvement and corporate donations.
• Strengthen our community by encouraging our leaders to serve in nonprofit and Chamber of Commerce leadership positions.

For additional information on Social Responsibility Strategies, refer to Table 7.3 and the Strategic Ideas section at the end of this chapter.

Congratulations!

You have completed 83 percent of your business planning process.
    If you would like to go deeper on your Strategies, continue reading.
    To take the shortcut, go to Chapter 9.

Case Study: Jack Stack Barbecue—
Strategies: The Major Categories of Work to Be Done

JOE: Once you had updated your vision, mission, and values, and defined your measures of success, how did you then create your strategies?

CASE: We came together as a team to form our strategies. We took the information that we had available to us including the SWOT (Strengths, Weaknesses, Opportunities, and Threats) analysis, Organizational Health Assessment (OHA), and results from our managers' surveys. We applied the 80/20 rule to determine the highest-leverage activities and the strategies that would have the greatest impact as we took our business to the next level. We want to maximize our resources to influence our organization as positively as possible.

JOE: Your two most important strategies related to Human Resources. What did you choose to name your first strategy?

CASE: Team Commitment. Over the past 10 years, our business had grown from a $5 million, single-unit operation with catering to a six-unit, multifaceted restaurant, shipping, and catering company. Communication was suffering and keeping our team engaged was getting increasingly difficult. It was clear that enhancing team commitment was the first and highest leverage activity that would create an immediate impact on our business. We established our team commitment strategy to improve the employee experience in our organization.

JOE: What end did you have in mind for your team commitment strategy? What categories of work did your team identify?

CASE: Quite simply, we wanted to improve employee satisfaction—which we decided to do through four specific areas of work.

1. **Consistent team engagement.** Though employee participation was strong at certain levels, it was inconsistent throughout the overall organization. We wanted to make it part of our culture to focus on it every moment of every day.

2. **Positive feedback.** We were hit between the eyes with the fact that although we truly make an effort to conduct positive activities like driving standards and our brand values within our business model, we weren't letting our team know what great work they were doing on a daily basis.

3. **Timely performance recognition.** We realized that we had to do more than just recognize positive contributions we had to provide timely performance recognition based on expectations and standards.
4. **Accountability.** We struggled with the last step of holding someone truly accountable, and the follow-up that was involved in doing this.

This led us to come up with our most important strategy:

Team Commitment: Improve employee satisfaction through consistent team engagement, positive feedback, timely performance recognition, and accountability.

It's clear. It's easy to communicate. And, most importantly, it's the right strategy for us.

JOE: What is your second strategy?

CASE: Human Resources. We are in the people business, and we feel that we're a unique member of the restaurant industry because of our values-driven team. We are looking for more than high performers or people with skills to do the work; we want our employees to share our values as well.

JOE: How did you define the end in mind here? What categories did you decide to work on?

CASE: We wanted to develop a values-driven, high-performing team with a focus on three specific areas:

1. **Effective hiring.** Bringing the right people on board is essential to moving our team forward.
2. **Proper placement.** Making sure that we have the right people performing the right jobs in our organization maximizes their— and the overall company's—success.
3. **Ongoing training.** This is continual development for all our people.

Our second strategy came together as the following:

Human Resources: Develop our values-driven, high-performing team through effective hiring, proper placement, and ongoing training.

JOE: How did you define your next strategy?

CASE: When we talk about what we do, produce, and sell as a company, it's more than food and service; it's our High-Value Experience. We want to consistently provide exceptional value through:

- **A clean environment.** From the moment a customer drives into the parking lot to the second they visit the restrooms, the environment must be clean and sanitary.
- **A hospitable atmosphere.** We want to make our guests feel as comfortable as possible at all times.
- **Extraordinary food.** We don't just want to serve fare that meets expectations, but food that leaves the customer remarking about it after they leave.

Our third strategy is:

High-Value Experience: Consistently provide exceptional value through a clean environment, a hospitable atmosphere, and extraordinary food.

JOE: You have two more strategies. What's next?

CASE: Productivity. We aim to maximize operational efficiency by:

- **Utilizing available resources and technology.** Selecting technology that really makes sense for us, and not just go after every tool that's available out there.
- **Developing effective and scalable systems.** Consistently developing our systems to make ourselves more efficient.
- **Streamlining communication.** Consolidate our communication so that employees know the quickest and easiest way to access information.

We are trying to maintain our edge in this challenging economy. We are in a position right now where we think we can gain market share, so it's important for us to maintain our presence in the market—and do a great job providing people access to and information about our products.

Our fourth strategy is:

Productivity: Maximize operational efficiency by utilizing available resources and technology, developing effective and scalable systems, and streamlining communication.

JOE: What final strategy did you identify?
CASE: Marketing and Sales. We realized that we could maximize sales volume by:

- **Creating raving fans.** We wanted to produce remarkable dining experiences that people will leave and tell their friends about— experiences that make them feel as though they can't wait to come back and do it again. This is the greatest asset that we have in our efforts to grow and propel our business forward.
- **Increasing brand synergy/awareness.** The goal here was to convert an out-of-state shipping customer to someone who would dine in our restaurant when in town. We also wanted to influence our dining customers to use our catering services for events, and so on.
- **Maintaining an integrated customer contact program.** We want to tie the data files for our shipping and catering program to the restaurants to create an integrated program that allows us to easily access all of our customer data from a single source.

Our fifth strategy is:

Marketing and Sales: Maximize sales volume by creating raving fans, increasing brand synergy/awareness, and maintaining an integrated customer contact program.

Ideas in Each of the Eight Strategic Categories to Help You Grow a More Productive and Profitable Business

1. Human Resources

McCown Gordon Construction has received numerous awards for their rapid growth and quality work. Shortly after developing their business growth plan, the *Kansas City Business Journal* recognized the company as one of the "Best Places to Work in Kansas City." They have received the award for the past five years. Pat McCown, CEO, attributes their high-trust and high-performing culture to selective hiring, employee engagement, and living their shared values.

Pat believes that businesses can no longer be competitive unless they engage every single team member. "By drawing out people's best ideas people feel valued, they have more buy-in, and our business makes better decisions."

McCown Gordon uses a process they call "Road Sign Mistakes" that encourages employees to openly share and learn from each other's mistakes. "People are making mistakes every day. We chose to consistently learn from them," says Pat.

"We have always sought to hire project managers who have strong leadership skills. Our clients love to have effective leaders helping them with their projects," Pat said. "Some companies display their values on the walls of conference rooms, while others may choose to talk about them. At McCown Gordon, our values shine through each team member and drive us to accomplish everything we achieve."

If you are developing and implementing a human resources strategy, you may want to consider some of these seven ideas.

1. "Hiring"—Are you hiring the right people?
   - Hire carefully, thoughtfully, and patiently.
     Often, past behavior is the best predictor of future behavior. Consider hiring a person who has successfully done the job in the past.
     Keep in mind that some of the most important job qualifications are extremely difficult to teach, such as ambition, intelligence, and character.
     There's a wise old saying that suggests you should "Hire slow and fire fast."
2. "Put the right people in the right positions."—Are the right people in the right jobs throughout your organization?
   - Match people's strengths and passions with their work assignments.
     Imagine how a winning baseball team would function if all the players switched positions. The catcher plays shortstop, the pitcher plays right field, and the first baseman pitches. There are two big problems with this scenario: first, the players won't enjoy their jobs; and second, the team will not perform as well as it could. Effective teams have complementary

strengths and share a common vision, mission, values, objectives, and strategies.

3. "Leadership"—Are you effectively leading and communicating with your team?

   • Help people connect their work with your business growth plan.

   Many employees feel that their work doesn't matter. Effective leaders help employees connect their daily work to the organization's vision and mission.

   In his book, *The Four Obsessions of an Extraordianry Executive*, Patrick Lencioni asserts that leaders must create and overcommunicate organizational clarity. People have a tendency to forget what they should remember, and remember what they should forget.

   By overcommunicating, employees gain a clearer understanding of how their work connects to the bigger picture, the business growth plan. This connection provides motivation, meaning, and focus that lead to higher performance.

   Remember, communication involves speaking and listening. Some of the most respected leaders and managers are really good listeners.

4. "Training"—Are people being trained to do their jobs?

   • Help people develop the skills they need to effectively do their job.

   Many companies are afraid to train people beyond their current skill level for fear that the employee will leave the organization. The bigger problem, however, is failing to train employees—and then having them *stay*.

   Many managers claim that the main reason for poor performance is their employees' lack of motivation, while many employees say the main reason for poor performance is not knowing how to do their jobs correctly.

5. "Management"—Are people being managed effectively?

   • Provide people with clear expectations and ongoing feedback on their performance.

   Two of the biggest reasons for poor employee performance are:

   1. People don't know what's expected of them.
   2. People don't know how they're doing.

This doesn't mean that managers need to micro-manage; they simply need to make it clear to their staff what their responsibilities are, how these efforts affect the company as a whole, and how well they're completing the tasks required of them.

6. "Incentives"—Are people being incentivized to perform at the highest levels?
   - Incentives must be meaningful for the employee and focused on the right outcomes. Incentives, like all matters of compensation, must be fair.

     In his book, *The Greatest Management Principle in the World,* Michael LeBoeuf writes, "You get more of the behavior you reward. You don't get what you hope for, ask for, wish for or beg for . . . . Come what may, you can count on people and creatures to do the things that they believe will benefit them the most."

     In other words: Employees will do their jobs to the very best of their ability when they're given reasons for doing so. Incentives can include acknowledgments like salary increases, enhanced benefits, bonuses, a positive work environment, and/ or perks like extra vacation days or employee outings/events/ dinners.

7. "Recognition"—Are you recognizing people's achievements?
   - The best recognition is personalized and meaningful to the individual.

     Here are a few popular ways to recognize people's performance:
   - Private and public praise from the manager.
   - Special praise or attention from upper management.
   - Honors and awards at company functions.
   - Certificates, plaques, trophies, and gift cards.
   - A congratulatory note or a personal letter.
   - Charts that display individual and team performance.
   - Compliment cards.

2. Physical Resources

In the summer of 2002, the leadership team at Randy Reed Automotive developed its business growth plan. The team agreed to grow from one to three dealerships by the end of the decade. By 2010, the company had finalized its investment in three new physical locations. The Buick-GMC, Chevrolet, and Nissan dealerships provide a solid foundation for achieving their vision, "The Region's Leader for Automotive Excellence." The company also completed a state-of-the-art Collision Center with high-quality, environment-friendly water-based paints.

Randy points out that, "Physical resources make a statement about who you are—your brand—before customers ever experience your people." The company's physical resources strategy was as follows: "*Physical Resources:* Expand our operations through investments in new physical locations, technology, and equipment."

If you are developing and implementing a physical resources strategy, you may want to consider some of these four ideas.

1. "Technology"—Are you utilizing cost-effective technology?
   - Provide people with the technology and equipment to serve customers efficiently and effectively.

   Our world is driven by technology. When it's functioning effectively and efficiently, no one notices; but if it's not working well, it causes frustration and dissatisfaction for both customers and employees. Providing people with the technology to do their jobs easily and quickly increases customer satisfaction, employee morale, and job satisfaction.

2. "Physical space"—Are you providing the right physical space for your customers and employees?
   - Invest wisely in physical resources that enhance the customer experience.

   There are a couple of guidelines to remember when making investments in your physical space. First, invest in real estate and improvements that are nice, but not *too* nice. You want to make your customers feel comfortable without creating the impression that you have money to waste.

   Second, invest in physical resources that enhance the customer experience. Don't spend excessively on employee resources. Walmart founder Sam Walton was well-known for driving around in an old pickup truck. Even though he was the richest man in the world, Walton preferred to invest money in the customer experience rather than a new vehicle.

3. "Equipment"—Are you using the right equipment?
   - Equipment investments should be based on the highest and best use of capital.

     The questions of which technology, physical space, and equipment are necessary can be a significant one for any business. A highly effective businessman told the story about Frito-Lay and Federal Express. Both companies leased space, instead of buying space, in southwest Missouri. Frito-Lay chose to invest its financial resources in product development; Federal Express invested in upgrades to their airplanes. Both organizations invested in assets that enhanced the customer experience.

     A business owner in a capital intensive industry described his philosophy on equipment purchases as follows:
   - Involve the people who use the equipment in the purchasing decision. You make a better decision and the employee will take better care of the equipment.
   - Buy high-quality equipment at the right price and maintain it properly.

4. "Space Utilization"—Are you utilizing your space wisely?
   - Have enough space to serve your customers, but not *too much* space.

     In order to reduce costs and improve operational efficiencies, you may want to consolidate your space. Could you generate the same amount of revenues and profits with less space or by consolidating your space? Talk with your employees and get suggestions from them regarding this matter. Figure out what will work best for all stakeholders—customers, vendors, employees, and so on.

3. Financial Resources

In its first 15 years, FishNet Security grew from $200,000 to $300 million in revenue. In 2005, the company developed its business growth plan and, in that same year, FishNet's founder Gary Fish positioned the company to obtain $12 million in private equity investments, helping perpetuate his vision of continued growth and stability. In 2006, Fish led his organization through the successful acquisition of SiegeWorks LLC and True North Solutions Commercial Operations, making FishNet Security the largest private information security solutions provider in the United States. In 2007, Gary Fish led the company to another successful private equity investment of $100 million.

Gary says, "There are many reasons to seek financing. You may need additional funds to grow your business, by hiring more people or investing in infrastructure. You may be at a point where you want to take some chips off the table or sell your entire business. You may even think you have the next market-changing idea, but need money to make it happen. Whatever the reason, there are several types of financing and investors you could consider, depending on your situation.

"The type of company you have built, or want to build, determines the type of investments available to you. If you have created a 'lifestyle business' from which you pay yourself the profits, your options are limited. If you have a great idea and a solid management team, you have more options."

Most new businesses seek capital from family, friends, or angel investors. Fast-growth companies may obtain financing from banks, angel investors, private equity, or venture capital. During a recent conversation, Gary Fish offered the following ideas related to financing.

If you are developing and implementing a financial resources strategy, you may want to consider some of these five ideas.

1. "Bank Financing"—Would your business benefit from bank financing?
   - Banks usually offer a favorable rate of interest but are risk adverse.

   A strong banking relationship is *essential* for professional success. However, banks are risk adverse. They won't finance a "good idea" and don't care if you "think" you will make money in the future. A bank's primary criteria for lending you money are based on your financial statements and past performance. Banks are looking to invest in a sure thing. If you can obtain bank financing, you will not pay as much for the capital or give up as much control.

2. "Angel Investors"—Is your business a candidate for angel investors?
   - Angel investors are more tolerant on their investment timeline, but usually receive a larger return on their investment.

     Angel investors are typically private investors who have been successful in their own careers and have substantial resources to invest in other companies. Most angel investors believe that their money will help your company grow and their experience and contacts can be valuable as well. I like to call this "Smart Money." Angel investors typically don't have the time to help you run day-to-day operations. So, they must believe in the management team and your ability to grow the business. Angel investors are definitely looking to receive a larger return on their investment than other investment vehicles available to them.

3. "Private Equity"—Is your business sophisticated enough to attract private equity funds?
   - Private equity firms are more hands-on and can provide valuable resources to help you grow your business.

     Private Equity (PE) is primarily looking to invest in profitable companies with strong management teams. The valuation of your company is usually based on EBITDA (earnings before interest, taxes, depreciation, and amortization). PE groups have to believe that your company will increase three times (or more) in value over the next three to five years. PE groups are more hands-on and can provide valuable resources to grow your business. They must also believe that the management team has the ability and experience to grow the business. PE groups are investing money from multiple investors including private individuals, pension funds, college endowments, and even from other PE funds.

4. "Venture Capital"—Is your business best suited for venture capital?
   - Venture capital groups may bring in their own teams to run and grow your business.

     Venture Capital (VC) is a structured investment, much like Private Equity, which is better suited for early-stage or concept companies. VC firms are typically investing money from multiple sources and include successful individuals who believe their experiences are valuable to the company. VC groups must believe in the management team and are more willing to bring in their own teams to run and grow your business. Because VC firms are investing at an early stage they want much more for their money.

5. "Obtain a Line of Credit"—Do you have a convenient, affordable line of credit?

   • If you don't currently have a convenient line of credit, arrange for a line of credit with the best credit terms possible.

      Having a line of credit allows you to make a phone call or write a check to access needed capital. The best time to develop a line of credit is when business is good and you don't need the money. The *worst* time to establish a line of credit is when you desperately need the money.

      Establishing a line of credit prepares you for the tough times. When adversity strikes, you're already in enough trouble. You certainly don't need to deal with the additional stress of trying to obtain much-needed capital.

4. Innovation

United Heating, Cooling and Plumbing opened their doors for business in 1990. By the end of their first year, they had grossed $600,000 in revenue with five employees. In 2004, they developed their business growth plan. Cofounder, Joe Lambert explains, "The process helped us get out of a funk. We weren't growing like we wanted, and it seemed like the three owners were making all the decisions. Three years later, our business had grown by 50 percent." Joe attributes their growth and success to a spirit of innovation and service. "We've always tried to improve on the way we do our business. We're reinventing our business about every three months. Then, our competition copies us and we find new and better ways to improve ourselves again. For example, during the recent housing downturn we strengthened our service business. Today, in the midst of the 'green movement' we've introduced new environmentally conscious options for our customers. Every business survives and thrives by staying on the cutting edge of change."

If you are developing and implementing an innovation strategy, you may want to consider these two questions.

- How can you improve your products and services?
- How can you develop new products and services?

Famed management expert Peter Drucker once said that innovation and marketing are the two essential strategies for any business. In other words, a company must consistently improve its existing products and services, while constantly developing new ones—and successfully bring those products and services to market.

Dr. Steve Gradwohl is the owner of Optimal Health Center, whose mission is "Optimal Health for Every Patient." Steve says, "We're always looking for new, cost-effective ways to fulfill our mission. Our latest innovation offers laser treatment for certain injuries. It's fast, it works, and it's cost-effective. We've learned that we can't fear failure. We make our best educated decisions regarding new products and services and if they are not effective, we make another more educated decision." Steve concludes, "We're here to serve our customers. The only constant is change. If we don't consistently adapt, our business will die."

Peter Drucker suggests that innovation can be defined in the way that French economist J.B. Say defined entrepreneurship. In 1804, Say claimed, "The entrepreneur shifts economic resources out of an area of lower productivity into an area of higher productivity and yield." Without innovation, every business ceases to exist.

5. Marketing and Sales

Earlier in the book, you learned about Joe Wilson and his team at Wilson Auctioneers in Hot Springs, Arkansas. After they defined their vision "To become the premier real estate auctioneers in Arkansas," the next question was: How do we get there? The answer to that question defined their strategy. Their most important strategy was "*Marketing:* Conduct higher quality real estate auctions by rebranding, television advertising, and selective selling." Joe's average real estate selling price grew from $80,000 to more than $200,000 in the first year. By holding fewer but larger real estate auctions, they were able to double revenues in that year. Wilson Auctioneers is focused on its passion and what the company does best. Their strengths and passion drive financial performance.

Marketing is the process by which you get prospects to contact you, whereas sales convert those prospects into customers. Both marketing and sales focus on creating an expectation that the customer will receive a desired benefit from doing business with you. That expectation is your brand—a promise you make.

Marketing and Sales seek to achieve four outcomes:

1. To have current customers buy more of your current offerings.
2. To have current customers buy new offerings.
3. To have new customers buy current offerings.
4. To have new customers buy new offerings.

If you are developing and implementing a marketing and sales strategy, you may want to consider some of these six ideas.

1. "Determine Your Ideal Customer"—Who is your ideal customer?
  • Describe in detail the characteristics of your ideal customer.
     Every business and marketing initiative starts by answering three questions:
     1. Who is your customer?
     2. What value will you provide for your customer?
     3. How will you deliver that value?
     It may also be helpful to ask, "Who is your *ideal* customer?" For example, the ideal customer for our business growth services is a business leader who wants to develop a higher performing organization, shares our business philosophy, and has a leadership team that wants to grow. Our marketing and sales efforts focus on reaching that person.
     Many organizations have a primary customer—a person whose life is improved by doing business with you—and a secondary customer, whose needs must also be satisfied. For example, our primary customer is the business leader, while our secondary customer is the employee that he or she leads.

2. "Understand Customer Wants and Needs"—What does your customer value?
   - Talk directly to your customers—past, present, and future—to discover their wants and needs.

     Peter Drucker spent the later years of his career working in college-level education. Each year, he personally phoned a random sample of 50 to 60 students who had graduated a decade earlier and asked, "Looking back, what contribution did this school make to your life? What do you still value today? What could we do better? What should we stop doing?" The answers to these questions helped him understand his customer's wants and needs.

3. "Database Management"—Are you developing your database?
   - Maintain an accurate, efficient, and effective database.

     Customer and prospect data is one of the most valuable assets for any organization. It is critical to have a database that captures and stores interactions and transactions with your customers and prospects.

     Be sure to capture all sales and service activity from your customers. This allows you to observe consumers' buying behaviors, and proactively sell products and services that are well suited to their needs.

4. "Marketing Message"—What is your brand promise?
   - Each employee should internalize and express your brand promise: your marketing message.

     Every company has a value proposition that tells your customer how your product or service will provide unique value. In many ways, your mission statement is like a value proposition. For example, Ritz-Carlton Hotels' motto is, "Ladies and gentlemen serving ladies and gentlemen." This is the expectation they create and deliver to meet their customers' wants and needs.

     Your brand promise separates you from the competition and solidifies customer loyalty.

5. "Marketing Communication"—What communication channels will you use? How often will you communicate?
   - Develop and implement a plan to communicate effectively with your customers and prospects.

Once you have determined your marketing message, it's time to select the best methods by which to communicate that message to your customers and prospects. These methods can include both direct and mass markets. Direct channels let you know exactly who you're talking to and include techniques like e-mail, direct mail, social media, telemarketing, and so on. Mass channels are a means by which you talk to everyone and anyone, such as via your website, magazines, newspapers, TV, and radio. You will want to design a marketing communication plan that will allow multiple touches to the prospect, preferably across various kinds of communication channels.

6. "Needs-Focused Selling"—Are you utilizing needs-focused selling to fulfill customer needs and wants?
- Be sure that your sales and service people are utilizing needs-focused selling techniques.

If you don't understand and meet customer wants and needs, then somebody else will. Therefore, you must employ sales and service people who have been trained to listen to the customer and respond to what they want and need. If your employees don't listen, they'll miss the mark when they recommend products and services.

People will buy what they want; if you cannot provide it, they'll find it somewhere else. Needs-focused selling is driven by a strong desire to serve others more than a desire to serve your own needs. Of course, by serving others, you best serve yourself.

6. Productivity/Delivery

WGK Engineers & Surveyors is a consulting engineering firm committed to providing superior quality professional services to promote the success of its clients. The company has enjoyed growth and success by maintaining personal and professional integrity, providing consulting services responsive to its clients' needs, fostering the personal and professional development of its staff, and improving its work processes.

The WGK business growth plan focused on improving a wide range of processes including billing, project management, budgeting, surveying, management, and human resources. "We were able to increase our profits by 400 percent in one year. Doing the right work with the right people in the right way has made all the difference," said Jeff Knight, founding principal.

If you are developing and implementing a productivity/delivery strategy, you may want to consider some of these five ideas.

1. "Customer Service"—Is your team focused on serving the customer?
   - It's fairly simple: *Serve your customers.* Pay attention to them, and solve their problems. It costs about 10 times more to find a new customer than to keep an existing one.

     Customer service is the one place where you can win a customer for life—or lose them along with four or five of their friends.

     General Motors surveyed customers who had owned a "Chevrolet" vehicle for a number of years. The company asked, "Would you continue to buy a car from us if it was priced like this or if it had these kinds of amenities, and so on?" The shocking result was that 85 percent of these loyal customers would switch; 5 percent would not switch; and the other 10 percent was neutral. What were the differences among the groups? The 5 percent of responders who said that they'd never switch had reasons regarding the customer service they'd experienced. It had little to do with product quality.

     Although a customer service process needs to be systematic, it must also be able to handle deviations that allow employees to personalize it when appropriate. You must make sure that you're meeting everyone's needs and keep in mind that not everybody is able to be accommodated by a "cookie cutter" approach.

2. "Standards of Performance"—Are you setting and monitoring standards of performance?
   - You must "inspect" what you "expect."

     It's important to provide feedback on performance throughout your organization. You should be evaluating and monitoring performance on an ongoing basis. Assess individual and team performance according to your values and performance criteria.

Standards of performance may be extremely detailed depending on the job, the type of business, and the size of the organization. Standards of performance may include safety, quality, budget considerations, regulatory requirements, timeliness, and accuracy.

Provide positive feedback when performance standards are exceeded. Provide objective feedback and specific suggestions for improvement when standards are not achieved.

3. "Improve Workflow Systems"—Are you improving workflow systems (processes)?
   - Ask yourself two questions: "Are we doing the right things?" and "Are we doing things right?"

     First of all, determine if you're taking the correct kinds of actions and that you're not wasting time. Once you do this, you then need to discern whether you're doing them the right way. You can't have a big month or a big year if you are constantly finding a bottleneck every time you start to get busy. You have to be able to run faster when the opportunity arises. If you can't, then you've hamstrung your organization and you're never going to get to the next level.

     Process improvement guru W. Edwards Deming said, "If you can't describe what you are doing as a process, you don't know what you're doing." The more you involve people in process improvement, the higher levels of commitment they will display.

4. "Process Literacy"—Is your team developing process literacy?
   - Equip your team with process knowledge so they can do their job with excellence.

     Every business has a wide range of processes, also called systems. Processes are simply the steps you take to accomplish the work that people do every day. As people work "in the system," they can also work "on the system."

     As your team develops process literacy, the people who do the work—who know the most about the job—can improve efficiency. They may need a little coaching to come up with a better system than how they're currently doing it—but you'll figure out something together that works best for everyone involved.

Systems lead to higher productivity, lower costs, higher profits, enhanced company value, and greater security for everyone in the company.

5. "Post-Delivery Reviews"—Are you conducting post-delivery reviews?
   • Ask for feedback and act on it.

   Business strategist Arie DeGeus said, "The ability to learn faster than your competition may be the only sustainable competitive advantage." Post-delivery reviews are an opportunity to learn from both your customers and employees on how to improve your delivery process in the future.

   It's not enough to simply ask for someone's feedback; you must take action on it. Before you can act on it, you must also ask the right questions—and listen to the answers. Simply asking for their ideas will prompt them to tell you how to make the experience better; and most of the time, their suggestions are not that complicated. "What worked?" (Do it next time.) "What didn't work?" (Eliminate it.) "What needs to be improved?" (Find a way to make it better next time.)

7. Profit Requirements

Businesses should be unapologetic about making reasonable returns on their investment.

Cary Summers has led three different companies during his career: Abercrombie & Fitch, Bass Pro Shops, and Silver Dollar City. His current company, the Nehemiah Group, consults on theme-park development projects around the world.

"When it comes to financial performance," Cary says, "only one thing really matters: and that's return on investment. In any company, there has to be a fair and equitable profit. A lot of leaders aren't paying attention to those activities that will generate profit."

Return on investment (ROI) is a universal principle. Everyone rightly expects a return on an investment—and this applies to all types of investments. People want to know: If I work here, what's my return on investment? If I engage in this relationship, what's my return on investment? If I invest in this particular enterprise, what's my return on investment?

Profit provides at least three useful benefits:

1. Profit measures business performance. It tells you how you are performing relative to previous years and your competitors.
2. Profit provides capital for future innovation and growth.
3. Profit is the return on investment required to stay in business. Not all years are profitable. Retained earnings provide the cash that keep a business from having to borrow.

If you are developing and implementing a profit requirements strategy, you may want to consider some of these five ideas:

1. Develop a "Financial Plan"—Are you developing an annual financial business plan?
   - If you don't have a clear financial plan to grow your business, create one as soon as possible. Get help if you need it.

      Financial knowledge, understanding, and wisdom are required to run a profitable business. The financial plan for your business should include three basic tools:

      1. Profit and Loss Statement
      2. The Balance Sheet
      3. Cash Flow Statement

      Many business leaders regularly forecast and monitor these three financial statements.

      Billionaire businessman and philanthropist Ewing Kauffman once told me that he always created three different scenarios when developing his financial plan.

      1. "Sure"—Your minimum expectations, be prepared for the worst.
      2. "Probable"—Your realistic expectations.
      3. "Possible"—What if things go *really* well, be prepared for this as well.

      When developing your budget, you will benefit from contingency planning.

2. "Hire a CPA"—Are you working with a competent CPA?
   - A competent CPA should be viewed as an investment, not an expense.

     Your business will become increasingly complex as it grows—so make sure that this complexity doesn't outgrow your CPA's competency. A skilled CPA will ensure you understand your financial statements. The day that you don't understand any number on your financial statements is the day you need to start asking your CPA more questions.

3. "Partner with a Banker"—Are you partnering with a competent banker?
   - Develop a trusted relationship with a competent commercial banker.

     It's important to have a quality banking relationship in *any* economy. Choose a capable, experienced commercial banker who is connected to a reputable bank—a banker who will get to know you and your company. There will be many times when you will want a banker who will go the extra mile for you.

4. "AP/AR Process"—Are you implementing an effective Accounts Payable and Accounts Receivable process?
   - Pay and collect your bills on time. This is an essential discipline for your ongoing reputation and financial performance.

     Virtually every business has honesty or integrity as one of their core values. Paying your bills on time demonstrates these values and builds trust with your stakeholders. It's equally important to make sure that you are managing your accounts receivable as efficiently as possible.

     When a business is growing, cash flow can be the biggest challenge.

5. "Financial Literacy"—Are you teaching financial literacy to your team?
   - Teach your team members the financial aspects of your business. They'll appreciate how the work they do contributes to the overall success of your enterprise.

     When Dr. Gregg Raymond and his team at the Center for Cosmetic Dentistry developed their business growth plan, their mission was defined as "Changing lives . . . a smile at a time." Gregg took a bold step and shared the company's financial information with his team. "It was scary," Gregg admitted. "I had never been so transparent with them. My team was surprised by what they learned, and I was surprised by their strong desire to help me build a better practice. My openness built trust and commitment. We were able to communicate at a higher level about our business objectives and our performance."

As your team members learn financial literacy, they also learn about your business. They come to see what it takes to build a more profitable and sustainable business.

Free market capitalism works better when more people understand how free enterprise works and the role they play in it.

Here are some other thoughts on profit:

Profit is not the legitimate purpose of business. The legitimate purpose of business is to provide a product or service that people need and do it so well that it's profitable.

—James Rouse, Entrepreneur and Philanthropist

Profit in business comes from repeat customers, customers that boast about your product or service, and that bring friends with them.

—W. Edwards Deming, Author, Lecturer, and Consultant

I don't want to do business with those who don't make a profit, because they can't give the best service.

—Richard Bach, Author

---

8. Social Responsibility

Rogers Strickland is the owner of several organizations, including Strickland Construction, Attic Storage, and Strickland Farms. Early in his business career, Rogers developed a strategy to give his leadership and financial resources to a wide range of charitable organizations. Rogers' legacy now includes 55 orphanages as well as several churches and community centers on four different continents. After a tragic 2007 tornado in Greensburg, Kansas, Rogers and his team were the first organization to rebuild a food pantry and thrift store on Main Street. Rogers explains, "Our legacy is the impact we make on those less fortunate. It's imperative for successful business owners to give, because we've been entrusted with so much. In other words, to whom much is given, much is required."

If you are developing and implementing a social responsibility strategy, you may want to consider these four ideas from several successful business leaders.

1. "Donating"—Are you making cash and/or noncash donations?
   - Give and you will receive.

     Consider the following words from some prominent company leaders:

     "My donations are led by my heart. I give where I have a passion to make a difference to people and organizations. I always receive more than I give in terms of my personal satisfaction and joy."

     "Our company tries to say 'yes' as much as possible. Even if it's just a small gift, it's our preference to help when we can."

     "We often leverage our giving power by donating products and services that have a high value to the charity and a low cost to our organization."

2. "Partnering"—Are you partnering with a charity?
   - Consider adopting a charity.

     Though charities certainly need funds, many organizations are moving away from just giving money and moving toward being *involved* in the charity—donating time and effort in addition to dollars. Over the past 20 years, the thinking has shifted from, "I'll write you the check," to "I'll write you the check if I can play in the game with you."

It's important to understand that charities and nonprofit organizations run differently from businesses. You have to be careful about what you expect from nonprofits, because their culture is different. Their people, the pace at which they make decisions, and the way they take action differs as well. You must be prepared to serve in their culture. You can impact the culture too, but be patient, understanding, and respectful.

3. "Leadership"—Are you providing leadership to your community?
   - If you have the time, leadership skills, and a passion to make a difference, partner with a nonprofit or community organization that wants your leadership.

     Our culture has developed a "leadership vacuum." Since companies generally cultivate leaders, any gift of leadership that you or others have could help a nonprofit organization in significant ways. If you can afford the time to do so, it's a great thing to do. You enhance the organization's ability to accomplish what they are trying to achieve by offering the leadership skills that you have developed in the business environment.

4. "Employee Involvement"—Are you involving your team in service activities?
   - Encourage your employees to engage in service activities.

     Case Dorman, from Jack Stack Barbecue says, "It's great to have your employees involved in service projects. Through their contributions, they learn that it's more blessed to give than receive, they develop their leadership skills, and they make a positive difference in our world."

     "At the end of each year, usually around Thanksgiving, we send a summary of our giving to the team. It says, 'These are the groups that we've helped; and this is the money and time that we put back into our community this year.' I do it for them so that they can understand that they are giving back to our community just by being a part of our team."

CHAPTER

Priorities

Who Will Do What by When? (10 minutes)

The key is not to prioritize what's on your schedule, but to schedule your priorities.

—Stephen R. Covey, Author

Don't be a time manager, be a priority manager.

—Denis Waitley, Author

Priorities are the specific tasks to be accomplished by individuals. Priorities are important, but usually not urgent. Priorities may include goals to achieve, problems to solve, or capacities to develop.

141

The Power of Priorities

Kelly Schoen is the CEO of award-winning direct marketing company Z3 Graphix. Z3 has a clear and compelling mission statement: "Helping our customers find more customers." Their strategies focus on building a high-performing team, improving operational efficiency, and increasing revenues.

Denise is Z3's customer service manager. She is responsible for implementing priorities relating to achieving high levels of customer satisfaction. Denise has a high capacity for detail and complexity. She's organized, and naturally thinks in terms of higher levels of efficiency.

Kelly and Denise worked together with the executive team to get on the same page and achieve their priorities. The result? "In our first three months, we accomplished more than we had in the previous two years combined," Kelly said. "Every month, our leadership team would meet to celebrate progress and set new priorities. The cycle of setting, achieving, and celebrating priorities on a monthly basis made all the difference." Denise recently reported achieving 47 high-leverage priorities in 14 months.

Why Write Priorities?

Priorities are the missing element of most business growth plans.

Priorities provide:

- Focus for people to achieve the important tasks to grow your business.
- An opportunity for people to enhance their competence, character, and confidence.
- Specific actions to deal with your organizational issues.

How to Write Priorities

Here is a four step process for writing effective priorities.

- **Start with a verb.** The best verbs show complete actions. "Finish," "complete," and "debrief" are better verbs than "study," "manage," or "help."

- **Make it measureable or observable.** Here's the question you need to ask: Can you tell when the priority is done? If not, it's not specific enough. You can tell if a priority that starts with "make recommendations" is finished; you can't if it starts with "study." If you know when something is completed, then you also know how much progress you've made.
- **End with a date.** To establish a high-achievement culture, you must be in the habit of putting dates on actions. Without a date, how can you prioritize the action steps or have any form of accountability? The little habit of putting dates on agreements can literally, all by itself, transform a low-performing culture to a higher-performing one.
- **Assign a priority to one person.** That doesn't mean one person does all the work; it just means that one person is responsible for seeing that the work gets *done*.

See Table 9.1.

Table 9.1   How to Write Priorities—Examples

1—Start with a verb	2—Make it measurable or observable	3—End with a date	4—Assign to a person
Hire	a new salesperson	by May 24	Melissa
Upgrade	the website	by June 12	Billy
Schedule	the employee service day	by November 25	Andrea

Table 9.2   Priorities Must Be Clear and Measurable

Unclear, not measured priority	Clear, measureable priorities
Launch new direct mail campaign by March 31.	Achieve a 10% increase in direct marketing leads by March 31.
Research new products for next fiscal year.	Make new product recommendations to leadership team by November 12.
Send Jim to consumer products convention in December.	Debrief consumer products convention at our team meeting by January 31.

Exercise 3:2 Write Your Priorities

Write on Table 9.3 the three to five most important priorities you need to accomplish in the next 30 days and transfer them to your business growth plan. See Table 7.3 in Chapter 7 for more examples.

Table 9.3

1—Start with a verb	2—Make it measurable or observable	3—End with a date	4—Assign to a person

---

Congratulations!

You have completed your business growth plan.

If you would like to go deeper on Your Priorities continue reading.

To write Action Plans, turn to Chapter 10.

Case Study: Jack Stack Barbecue Priorities—Who Will Do What by When?

Interview with Rod Toelkes, Director of Operations, Jack Stack Barbecue

JOE: What has this planning process done for you and your team?

ROD: I've seen some really good progress in our stores. I'll be honest with you—I've struggled a little bit with the accountability of my general managers for quite some time. I attribute a lot of that struggle to the fact that they're pretty new at their positions in this industry. And I am very strict about my standards-driven style of management.

This planning process has really helped me lead our GMs and managers. Our structure, time management, accountability, and follow-through are all improving. We have finally been introduced to a system that truly keeps our daily, weekly, and monthly focus on what's really important in our operations.

I could sit here and talk all day about how to operate a business—but none of it means anything without the strengths, talents, and personalities of the people who really make a company what it is. And our people are better because of this process.

JOE: Can you provide an example of where you see greater accountability?

ROD: I can honestly say that in all four of our restaurants we have accomplished 40 percent to 50 percent more in the projects and priorities completed in the past two months than in the previous six months combined.

JOE: How has this happened?

ROD: We have learned the power of focusing on activities that are important, whether they are urgent or not. We used to spend so much time discussing all kinds of issues; now we focus on the ones that are really critical to all of us. As you say, we are on the same page and achieving "Quadrant 2" priorities (important, but not urgent). It's working.

JOE: What about Bryan and his progress as a new GM?

ROD: Bryan has greatly improved his ability to focus and prioritize since becoming a general manager. He also excels in terms of his people skills, personality, the way he carries himself, and how deeply he cares for his teams. He's the type of individual that connects with people very easily through his kind heart and gentle yet outspoken manner. He is a very understanding individual, and the kind of guy that I always knew would be a GM someday.

Bryan was always willing to work hard; he simply wasn't always sure about the kind of work he should be doing. Bryan is also the ultimate note taker, and his listening skills are excellent. Before this process, he would struggle with accountability and time management because he didn't effectively prioritize his notes. This planning process has really enabled him to structure his note taking, projects, people-development classes, and things of that sort. It has pretty much narrowed things down for him—and for all of us. We can talk about thousands of projects in our restaurants, literally, on a weekly basis. But this has really enabled us to narrow the list down to the *truly* important things.

Interview with Bryan Davis, General Manager, Jack Stack Barbecue

JOE: What has this planning process meant to you?

BRYAN: It's enabled me to bring the pieces together regarding how I manage my restaurant . . . and has set the accountability portion in place. The process keeps me moving forward. It gets rid of a lot of the daily "fluff," and keeps me focused on what I'm doing and what I'm trying to achieve.

JOE: It sounds like you now have a more systematic way of determining what's important and what's not.

BRYAN: In the past, even if I *did* think something was important, it might not have been *urgent*. So it got lost in the sea of everything else and I got lost in the minutia, wrapped up in the day-to-day operations. I just wanted to make sure the guests were taken care of, and I wasn't moving forward as a leader.

JOE: Tell me some things in your restaurant that are very important to you, that help you move forward.

BRYAN: Right now, my key thing is working with my managers, getting us all on the same page and having us work together so that we don't create any kind of triangulation with our staff. I want my managers to be moving forward with me. And that doesn't mean that they have to be on *my* page, necessarily; it could be their page, as long as we can work together. There's open discussion about it.

JOE: You're obviously very committed to your people. You want to engage their best efforts and their best thinking. What's your mind-set regarding your direct reports, your management team?

BRYAN: I basically divide the restaurant up. It's about giving them the empowerment to realize, "Hey, I own this piece of the business.

I'm running this. I'm telling my boss what's going on, and I'm proud of it. Therefore, I'm going to do the very best I can to make sure that I've got my areas of responsibility handled."

JOE: I see. In a sense, you give them the responsibility to be their own "Mini-GMs."

BRYAN: Exactly. And the one great thing I've found going through this is that it's not a negative accountability; it's an accountability piece that was established by my managers because they have a great sense of pride in owning their own area.

JOE: Tell me about the kinds of day-to-day operations that can be so consuming in this business.

BRYAN: Last Saturday morning from 9 to 10 AM, we got our entire team together for an all-employee meeting. Later that day, approximately 35 employees served over 1,000 customers. It's our job as a management team to make sure we have the right people, great food, and all the other parts of the business working effectively to create the guest experience. Serving over 1,000 guests was a big day for us, and it was the first day our outdoor patio was full all night as well.

JOE: What are some of the Quadrant 2 (important and not urgent) priorities that you've been able to accomplish in the past couple months?

BRYAN: In addition to encouraging our management team and employees to collaborate more closely, I've been investing more time in improving our Quality Circle Meetings. These gatherings engage our employees and managers in an open dialogue about how to improve our business.

Another high-priority item is training the trainers. We're making sure we have the right people in those positions, giving them the tools to train more effectively, and creating a stronger sense of accountability between the trainers and staff.

JOE: What else are you working on?

BRYAN: I am retraining my managers on progressive discipline, and it's really opening up some eyes for my managers. There are always some people who say, "Oh, you've got to write them up!" But, it's not about that; it's about sitting down and figuring out what the problem is together. Honestly, a lot of my success comes from being able to talk to people, listening to what they have to say, putting myself in their shoes and really getting down to the bottom of it. I want my managers to know that this is a tool to better our staff; it's not an excuse to sit down and chew somebody out.

JOE: Someone once told me that, "You should never give an employee any feedback unless the feedback will help them improve their performance." That's what you're doing.

BRYAN: We're also letting neighboring businesses and hotels know that we appreciate their referrals to Jack Stack, and we're providing coupons for concierges and customers.

JOE: How has your focus on Quadrant 2 priorities changed the way you lead your team?

BRYAN: In the past, my managers would often come to me and ask what to do—which used to take a lot of my time. I would let them pull me in and make decisions for them. Instead, I now say, "What are *you* going to do about it?"

They have developed an attitude that says, "I can and will make decisions."

We are also using your "compliment cards" to build trust and relationships among our team. It is a great feeling to receive a compliment card; it recharges your battery and pulls you out of any negative place you might be in. It made me feel really good to compliment my managers and see them take my comments to heart. Maybe I just don't know how to take praise very well, but I actually find it more satisfying and uplifting to compliment others.

JOE: Any other experiences of what it's been like to go through this process?

BRYAN: As I mentioned previously, my to-do list is a lot shorter and much more focused. It's also impacted my personal life. You really hit me with your driveway story. Now, I pull into my driveway at the end of the day and say, "This is where my most important work begins." That is incredibly important to me. I make sure that no matter how tired I am, I recharge my battery a little and spend time with my wife. I'm going to be with her the rest of my life, and I've got to take care of her. It's really showed me the importance of setting priorities that are in Quadrant 2 at home as well, to better my entire life.

JOE: What are some of the Quadrant 2 priorities that you and your wife are able to accomplish?

BRYAN: We started by getting our finances in order. With a clear budget and spending guidelines, our finances are able to pretty much run themselves. We also want to develop a stronger relationship with our foster daughter, Alyssa. She just turned nine years old and is getting some professional help for her issues. Rebecca and I are committed to helping Alyssa live a better life.

The Key to More Effective Time Management

Here's the most important lesson I've ever learned about time management.

A college professor in the 1920s suggested that everything we do in life falls into one of four categories: important and urgent, important and not urgent, not important and urgent, and not important and not urgent. The actions we take are important if they contribute to our Vision, Mission, Values, Objectives, and Strategies or they're not important. These actions are urgent if there is an implication of time pressure, and not urgent if there's no time pressure.

The Time Management Matrix in Table 9.4 helps us understand how we can use our time more effectively.

Quadrant 1 entails matters that are important and urgent; an instance where your biggest client has a pressing need, your entire office's computers crash, or there's a deadline-driven project you need to complete. Quadrant 1 items get done.

Quadrant 2 items are important and *not* urgent. Everything you do that improves the quality of your work and life fits into Quadrant 2. Building relationships, working on personal development, seizing new opportunities, empowering others, preventing and preparing for problems, preparation, and engaging in better planning are all in Quadrant 2.

Quadrant 3 includes items that are not important but there's a sense of urgency. They're deceptive in that urgency feels like importance. For example, do you really need to check your e-mail as frequently as you do or does it take time away from more important work that you

Table 9.4 Time Management Matrix

	Urgent (time pressure)	Not Urgent (no time pressure)
Important (significant impact on your plan)	1. These activities usually get done.	2. These activities are high impact. Make them a priority.
Not Important (insignificant impact on your plan)	3. These activities are deceptive, don't confuse urgent and important. Minimize these activities.	4. These activities are a waste of time. Avoid them.

could be doing? Many e-mails, phone calls, and meetings are not necessarily important, because they don't contribute to your Vision, Mission, Values, Objectives, and Strategies.

Quadrant 4 is not important and not urgent. These items waste your time. You might find yourself lost in cyberspace, with no mission to accomplish. Many time wasters and escape activities can be found in Quadrant 4.

Would it surprise you to learn that most people spend over half of their time in Quadrants 3 and 4?

To live an extraordinary life and build an extraordinary business, you must live above the line and focus on what's important.

By developing your Business Growth Plan, you and your team draw the line. *You* define what's important.

During the 1990s, I had the privilege of serving as a senior consultant with the Franklin Covey Company. I spent the entire decade helping people discover habits and principles of effectiveness that could improve their organizations and their lives. Stephen Covey told me that the most important advice he would give a person in the area of time management was to plan your week—*every* week—before it even begins. Likewise, *The One Hour Plan for Growth* helps you develop a business plan before you start investing your time.

What Happens When We Don't Prioritize?

Many years ago, I learned a valuable lesson about priorities. After a long international trip, I returned to my Kansas City office with a serious case of jet lag. I also returned to a large stack of items that required my attention. It was mid-afternoon, so I had several hours to get the work done. I was so tired, however, that without thinking, I began addressing the items one at a time from the top of the stack.

Most of us have heard of the "ABC Technique" for prioritizing the things we want to get done. You simply rate an item's importance with an "A," meaning that it needs to get done today; a "B," which means it would be *nice* to get it done today; or a "C," which signals that it is not necessary to get done today. The next two steps of the "ABC Technique" are to number and execute the priorities in their order of importance. For example, do A1 first, then A2, then A3, and so forth.

Well, knowing and doing are two entirely different things.

So imagine that large stack of items that required my attention, and picture me addressing the items one at a time from the top of the stack. Based on their real priority, it went something like this: B2, C5, A3, B10, A7, B4 . . . You get the idea. It wasn't until a little before 5 PM that I achieved my A2 priority. Finally, a little after 5 PM, I finally came to my A1 priority. But it was too late by then. The day was over. The unmade phone call cost me a significant business opportunity.

What a valuable lesson!

And too often, for too many of us, this is the way it goes. Without thinking through and identifying our priorities, individuals and organizations waste an incredible amount of time and underserve their customers, fellow employees, and business owners. A day, week, quarter, year, or a life may end without the A1 priority being accomplished.

As writer and philosopher Elbert Hubbard said, "It does not take much strength to do things, but it requires a great deal of strength to *decide* what to do." Your business and your life can be extraordinary when you take a few minutes or an hour to plan on a regular basis.

How Do You Keep Your Mojo Working?

Have you ever wondered what separates the climbers from the quitters? In other words—why are some people able to sustain high levels of motivation throughout their entire lives, while other people have a hard time getting out of bed and going to work in the morning?

Through my association with Ron Willingham—author of 12 books and pioneer in interactive training—I've learned that a person's achievement drive is the "multiplier" that makes the difference in individuals' and organizations' successes or failures. You know that a person's desire, drive, and ambition are fundamental to his or her success; but what many people don't know is that their achievement drive can actually work *against* them.

For instance, you know that if you try too hard to go to sleep, you might find yourself more wide awake. If you put undue pressure on yourself to perform exceedingly well, you might actually perform *worse* than usual. If you try to motivate yourself to accomplish a particular task, you might find yourself quickly losing energy. A high degree of motivation can be a blessing or a curse, depending on how it's used. Let me explain.

Think of yourself as a high-performance automobile, with a "starter" and a "motor." To consistently achieve at the highest levels you must understand the vital role that your starter and motor play in your achievements. The starter is designed to get the motor going and get the wheels turning. This is what puts the vehicle in motion. It was never intended, however, to propel the vehicle down the road; it was designed to be used only for short periods of time. If you run your starter for too long, you run the risk of wearing your battery down. The more you run your starter, the more you run down your battery—and the longer it takes for the battery to recharge. This is a problem for many people: in essence, they have an overused starter. Their batteries are run down. They no longer have the ability to get their motors revved up.

I've been exercising regularly for about 30 years. I can honestly say that most of the time I don't want to exercise. But, my starter gets me on the bike, in the pool, or in the gym. Then, almost every time, my motor takes over. I can only think of a few times out of thousands of workouts that the motor just didn't get started.

Many people burn out their starters by thinking too much about the energy required to complete the task. It's a counterproductive use of your mental energy. High achievers understand that the starter is only designed to get the motor running. Once the motor is started, it runs by itself.

In other words, the more you think about doing something rather than just doing it, the more you kill your Mojo. Propel yourself to begin, and then let the force of the task take over.

CHAPTER 10

Action Plans

Putting It on the Calendar and Getting It Done

The journey of a thousand miles begins with one step.
—Lao Tzu, Chinese Philosopher

He who every morning plans the transaction of the day and follows on that plan, carries a thread that will guide him through the maze of the most busy life. But where no plan is laid, where the disposal of time is surrendered merely to the chance of incidence, chaos will soon reign.
—Victor Hugo, Writer and French Statesman

The immature mind hops from one thing to another, the mature mind seeks to follow through.
—Harry A. Overstreet, Psychologist

The elevator to success is out of order.

You'll have to use the stairs . . . one step at a time
—Joe Girard, Author

An Action Plan is a list of specific steps with due dates to achieve a priority.

An action plan is simple and powerful. If achieving a priority is like climbing a mountain, the action plan details each individual step you must take. Although action plans won't fit on a business growth plan, they will provide the necessary clarity to take action, manage your time more effectively, and make progress.

Here's how it works: Action Plans help you achieve Priorities. Priorities help you achieve Strategies, and Strategies help you achieve your Vision.

Think about it. What are the steps you need to take?

See Table 10.1 for an example.

So much time is wasted every day because people do not know what to do next. The simple solution is to define your priorities, create action plans, and accomplish those items one at a time.

An action plan helps you make progress as you take the steps necessary to achieve a priority. It's so much easier to be productive when you are clear about what to do next. It's also very rewarding to check the items off your list.

The dates in an action plan are not always as critical as the date on a priority. (So what if you're a day or a week late in making the offer as long as the new sales manager can still start by February 1?) Think what power and imagination can be released in your organization when action items are clear.

Table 10.1 Achieving Your Vision Step by Step

Vision	To be the leading provider of office equipment in Minneapolis.
Strategy	Human Resources: Improve performance by getting the right people in the right positions, developing their talents, and managing them effectively.
Priority	Start new Sales Manager by February 1.
Action steps	☐ Advertise in three different places by January 3. ☐ Contact 10 business associates for referrals by January 5. ☐ Pick final candidates for interviews by January 10. ☐ Complete interviews by January 18. ☐ Make job offer by January 21. ☐ Welcome new Sales Manager on the job by February 1.

Action plans can help you provide the right amount of oversight for any project. Managers are often tempted to go to extremes: either micro-managing or abandoning employees. But a balance somewhere in the middle of these two approaches is the most effective method for developing employee accountability and trust. It's easy to review the actions on a regular basis and ask how it's going. The person responsible for implementing the action plan can then show how he or she is making progress. Not too much control—and just enough support and encouragement.

Action Plans Exercise 1

Choose a priority you can accomplish on your own and develop your action steps. In other words, everything "to do" will be yours to accomplish. See Table 10.2.

Table 10.2

PRIORITY:	
Action Steps	Completion Date

Action Plans Exercise 2

Choose a priority you will accomplish with others and develop the action steps. Some of the tasks here are yours to accomplish, and the others are your teammates' responsibilities. See Table 10.3.

Table 10.3

PRIORITY:		
Person Responsible	**Action Steps**	**Completion Date**

The $25,000 Planning Idea

Charles Schwab was president of Bethlehem Steel in the early twentieth century when he met with Management Consultant Ivy Lee to improve his company's productivity. "We know what we should be doing, and we want to do more of it," explained Schwab. "Show us a better way of getting it done and I'll pay you what it's worth."

In 20 minutes, Ivy Lee gave Charles Schwab the advice he requested. Lee handed Schwab a blank sheet of paper and said, "Write down the six most important things you need to accomplish tomorrow."

Then Ivy Lee said, "Now number them in their order of impor-tance." Lee continued, "Put the list in your pocket, and tomorrow morning, take out your list and go to work on the first item. Keep work-ing until the first item is completed. Then, work on other items, in or-der, until they are completed. You'll always be working on what is most important."

Lee then suggested that Schwab stay with this system, and teach it to others on his team. "Then," said Ivy Lee, "Send me a check for what-ever you think it's worth."

A few weeks later, Schwab sent Lee a check for $25,000 with a letter saying that it was the most profitable productivity idea that he had ever learned. Shortly thereafter, Bethlehem Steel became the largest indepen-dent steel company in the world.

According to a survey taken by Day-Timers, only one-third of U.S. workers plan their daily schedules; and only 9 percent actually follow through on these plans. To get more done in less time, define your pri-orities and the action steps needed to achieve them. Then, put your ac-tion steps onto your calendar—and simply enjoy being productive.

It's important to understand that some people get their best results by being more spontaneous and less structured. These people, me in-cluded, may not always achieve sequentially, but we still benefit by con-sistently focusing on what's important.

We cannot overestimate the positive impact of working with a team of people to accomplish the six elements of your business growth plan. Everyone on your team understands where you're going (vision), why you're going there (mission), and how you treat each other along the way (values). People also understand the measures of success (objectives) and the categories of work that must be accomplished (strategies) to grow your business. By the time people define priorities and action steps, there is a shared commitment, a positive support system, and genuine team work.

How to Get More Done in Less Time

As personal productivity guru, David Allen, writes in his book *Getting Things Done: The Art of Stress-Free Productivity*, the reason "something is on your mind" is that you want it to be different than it currently is, and yet:

- You haven't defined exactly *what* you want.
- You haven't decided the steps you need to take.
- You haven't put *reminders* of the steps in a system that will prompt you to do it.

That's why it's still "on your mind"; until you take these three steps, that's where it will stay. However, once you take those three steps, your mind is freed up to live in the moment and you enjoy making progress.

In today's ever-changing marketplace, leaders at all levels must be absolutely clear about what they want to achieve and the steps to achieve it. Then, of course, there needs to be a reliable system in place to ensure that your ideas turn into actions and results.

PART

Engaging Your Team

CHAPTER

What's Next?

How to Create and Execute a Team Plan for Years to Come

Inside every old company is a new company waiting to be born.
—Alvin Toffler, Writer and Futurist

A person must grow out of small problems to free up the energy to deal with bigger problems. That is the process of growing and maturing. The same applies to organizations.
—Ichak Adizes, *Corporate Lifecycles*

If the rate of change inside an organization is slower than the rate of external change—the end is near.
—Jack Welch, Former Chairman and CEO, General Electric

Engaging Your Team in the Planning Process

If you choose to engage your team in the process, and I hope that you do, you will experience the exhilaration of being on the same page and achieving extraordinary results that can only be achieved as people work together.

In order to engage the best efforts of today's workers, involve your team in this planning process. You *can* create a plan without any involvement from your team. But, you won't have as much buy-in. You know the principle: no involvement, no commitment.

Involving people in the planning process engages and develops their leadership skills and brings forth their best ideas.

When you ask for people's opinions, you make them feel important and give them a sense of ownership and commitment to the plan. And your plan is made stronger through their contributions. Of course, it is ultimately the leader's responsibility to develop a plan, but why not involve your people—the ones who are going to make it happen—in creating the plan?

Three Steps to Define and Achieve Your Team's Business Growth Plan

Follow these simple steps to get your team on the same page and achieve higher levels of performance.

1. **Assemble the right team(s).** Involve the right people at the right time in the process. Start with the leader, then the leadership team, then the management team—and eventually, the entire organization.
2. **Develop the Business Growth Plan annually.** Invest enough but not *too much* time in the process. An initial draft of your plan can be created in an hour or so by each of the leaders. In one day's time, the leadership team can get on the same page with shared vision, mission, values, objectives, strategies, plus individual priorities for each participant. You may want to use an outside facilitator to keep the process on track. You can usually run

an effective employee meeting to get your employees on the same page in about an hour.

3. **Celebrate your progress and set new priorities monthly.** The process of celebrating your progress, reviewing your plan, and setting new priorities sustains performance over time.

The following interview with Case Dorman will help you understand how this process works.

Case Study: The Jack Stack Story—Engaging the Team in the Planning Process

JOE: Let's talk about how you rolled this planning process out to your team.

CASE: We have four groups: our leadership team, our general managers, our store managers, and all of our employees. We thought it best to roll out the plan slowly to ensure buy-in at every level.

JOE: So you started with your leadership team?

CASE: We get together as a leadership team once a week for our operations meeting. This team of six people is basically the holding company that serves all the different business units; four restaurants, catering, and shipping. I had initially asked the leadership team to read your book and determine whether they felt the same way I did about your approach. I needed to find out if they felt like this was something that would help us be better at what we do.

I try to utilize the 80/20 Principle to avoid wasting time on something that is not going to be a long-term solution. I evaluate every system based on how complicated it will be to implement and the impact it will have on our business. We felt that this one was a good fit. We engaged in the initial planning process and after a very dynamic day together, we came away with a stronger sense of purpose, clarity, and focus.

JOE: Then you engaged the second group—your general managers.

CASE: We invited the general managers to join the leadership team and then we developed plans for each of their stores. It worked well to have a member of the leadership team work with each of the general managers to develop their Business Growth Plan. The day was well spent, and the process was well-received. It's also noteworthy that all of these participants had written and gone to work on their most important priorities.

JOE: Your third group is each store's management team.

CASE: All members of the leadership team visited each store meeting to share the new plan and help management understand it. We did this so that when we approached the team as a whole, the managers would already understand the plan and be engaged in the process. We wanted them to be comfortable with the way we would deliver to their team. The other thing that we did was have them all vote on the vision, mission, and values first.

JOE: What impact is the plan having on the GMs and their management teams?

CASE: One of the leadership team's greatest challenges is helping our business unit leaders—our GMs—develop their management teams. Because our company has grown pretty quickly, we were backfilling these leadership positions behind us with great "sergeants" that had not had much experience being "generals." We knew that the GMs would need to develop their management teams in order to reach their full potential; and we saw some gaps to fill in terms of how we could help them do that. We recognized this tool as a great opportunity to help the GMs help *their* management teams by developing them, holding them accountable, and encouraging their growth.

JOE: You, Travis, and the GMs met with the management teams to review their plans?

CASE: We kept getting more buy-in, and we built momentum as we included more people in the process.

JOE: Lastly—and perhaps most importantly—you met with the employees.

CASE: We went out to each of the stores and met for about an hour with all of our employees.

JOE: That's the meeting I attended last Saturday morning at the Plaza restaurant with Bryan's team. [For leaders who want to engage their employees with their Business Growth Plan, I've attached a summary of that meeting at the end of this chapter.]

So, you assembled your six teams of 540 total people and got them on the same page. How long did that take?

CASE: It took a couple of months to get 540 people on the same page in terms of the process.

JOE: Now it's time to make progress and celebrate that progress on a monthly basis. Tell us about that.

CASE: Our old meetings had become exhausting; we would emerge from them totally worn out. For the first time this week, I changed the style to the new format and we left that meeting energized. It had a much better feel to it and it was much more productive.

JOE: How long do your weekly leadership meetings last?

CASE: In the past, these meetings could run from three to four hours. Yesterday, we decided we would limit those meetings to 90 to 120 minutes—never going past two hours.

JOE: So, this process has not only made the meetings more energizing and effective but now you are able to save 50 to 70 hours of everybody's time every year. With a team of six members, that is a savings of 300 to 420 hours per year!

CASE: Yep, that's a chunk of time.

JOE: Do you have an agenda for the new 90- to 120-minute meetings?

CASE: It's basically the same agenda that we use in our monthly manager meetings; I've got it broken down into five sections.

1. **Success and Progress**—We review our priorities and celebrate the progress we've made and the success we've achieved.
2. **Lessons Learned**—We share stories about anything that has happened to the team in the past week from which we can all learn something.
3. **Business Review**—We review our financial statements and identify any opportunities for improvement.
4. **Operations**—We discuss our people and any operational issues— food, service, team—any problems that we need to work on.
5. **Set New Priorities**—We update our plan, as needed, and set new priorities for the next 30 days.

Everyone takes a turn in each section. They each get a few minutes to talk about their success and progress. We make sure that the team members keep it short—and the same is true with each of the other sections. It really has helped us pick up the tempo of the meeting. In the past we would go around the table and each individual would spend up to 40 minutes going through their entire list—which got stale, and somewhat draining.

JOE: How is the team progressing?

CASE: Our managers are changing the way in which they structure their time, their day, and their week. They're being better delegators and holding people accountable. I do think there is some significant benefit in the structure that is being honed in their leadership styles and their ability to hold others accountable.

We are also seeing bottom line results. We just finished our best month ever for sales and increased profitability by 50 percent for the month. This month is setting up to be a record month as well with same store sales up more than double our budgeted amount and profitability is strong.

Engaging Your Employees with Your Business Growth Plan

On a beautiful spring day in Kansas City, more than 70 team members gathered at Jack Stack's Barbecue Restaurant on the Country Club Plaza. The purpose of the meeting, announced Case Dorman, "is communication, and getting all of us on the same page, so we can make progress together." The meeting was fast-paced and involved three different presenters. Everyone was seated and attentive at 9 AM—and the meeting was over at 10 AM.

This Saturday morning gathering is a great example of leadership, how to conduct an effective meeting, and how to engage your entire team in the planning process. The following is a brief summary of the meeting that might help you lead your team in the years ahead.

Case Dorman, president of Jack Stack Barbecue, started the meeting with a prepared set of the flip-chart pages by stating, "The restaurant industry has changed dramatically in the past couple years. The upscale casual dining segment has gone from fast growth to a 20 percent loss of business in the past two years. At Jack Stack, our entire business is up about 8 percent in those two years and your store is already up 4 percent this year. You're doing a good job." (Applause)

"What's next?" Case asked. "Looking out 5, 10, 20 years—what do we want to become?" He continued, "All businesses—like all people—have life cycles. Companies are born; they grow, and eventually mature to achieve peak performance. Some mature faster than others; again, just like people." (Laughter) "If businesses don't continue to grow and improve, what happens?" Audience members replied, "They decline and might die."

Case continued, "Our business has gone through several restarts and growth phases since 1957 when Grandpa Russ opened his first barbecue restaurant in South Kansas City. Not too many restaurants or businesses last 50 years. So what's our vision for the next 50 years? We want to be 'The Nation's Premier Provider of Kansas City Barbecue.'"

Case went on to explain in detail what each of those words means (see Chapter 4, "The Customer-Centered Mission Statement"). He asked the group if anyone could recite the company's original mission statement. When no one could, he explained that the new vision, mission, and values statements would be much easier to remember. Case also explained the original mission statement with a passionate recommitment to the never-changing values that include treating our team with respect and our guests as family.

Case then passed the baton to Travis, Jack Stack's vice president, to talk about how and why the company was changing the mission statement. Travis explained to the group, "We'd like your feedback on several possible mission statements. Everybody needs to have a voice. We are going to vote." The room began to buzz as people reached for their pens, and every employee was handed a ballot. See Table 11.1.

FIORELLA'S
JACK STACK
BARBECUE

Table 11.1

Rank	Mission Statement Choice
____	Remarkable Barbecue Experiences
____	Creating Remarkable Barbecue Experiences
____	Creating Exceptional Barbecue Experiences
____	Create your own if you want:

After briefly explaining some of the discussions managers had been having, everyone voted. "Creating Remarkable Barbecue Experiences" was their first choice. After the meeting I looked at the ballots and saw a strong write-in vote for "Remarkable Barbecue—everyday."

Travis asked the group if they had ever been stopped by a "Raving Fan" while wearing their Jack Stack logo wear in public. He wanted to know, "What do they say?" Employees immediately replied, "I love that place!" "Cheesy Corn," "Burnt Ends." Travis said, "That's what we're about, being remarkable!"

"Let's talk about our values," Travis continued. "It's how we treat each other. It's how we treat our guests. I think values are the most important part of our business. They're vital, because they create trust. Good companies appreciate their employees and customers every day, and acknowledge your worth as a person." The team voted on their values. (Note: At Jack Stack Barbecue, all 540 employees have a shared vision, mission, and values. Each of the six business units have their own strategies and objectives.)

Travis turned the meeting back over to Case to review the results of their recent Organizational Health Assessment. Case started with a long list of positive results, which included an awareness of strengths, employees knowing what's expected of them, they maintain life/work balance, the store is a learning organization, and employees enjoy good relationships with their managers.

Case then acknowledged some of the challenges facing the company. He said that it was his fault that the store had changed general managers three times in four years, and he didn't like it. "But," he said, "We've got the right guy now." (Applause) Case said, "I'm not always quick, but I keep trying." (Laughter) Case identified a few specific areas that still needed improvement, including more direct communication, positive feedback, and accountability. Then, Case turned the meeting over to General Manager Bryan Davis.

Bryan started his short presentation on strategies by stating, "This planning process has helped me learn a very valuable lesson: I wear 20 percent of my clothes 80 percent of the time. (Laughter) And, likewise, I need to look at our restaurant and identify the 20 percent of activities that will create 80 percent of the impact on our future success." He went on to review each of the five strategies from the Plaza's business growth plan: Management Development, Team Commitment, Human

Resources, Operations, and Marketing/Sales. Bryan shared areas of work, including more one-on-one time to develop managers, more positive recognition of employees or conversations to discover how they see their future with the company, putting the right person in the right job, progressive discipline, and more day-to-day coaching for higher performance. Bryan also expressed his passion to improve carry out operations and sales, and announced a program to canvas area hotels, utilize $5 coupons and an American Express discount program.

Lastly, Bryan reviewed the store's objectives for the year. He encouraged participation in the Management Surveys and told people not to be afraid of Secret Shoppers. "Just keep doing your best," he said, "You're awesome!" He also explained the pit fork score and the annual Organizational Health Assessment, and announced the financial goals and progress made so far this year. Then Bryan turned to the audience for *their* input by asking, "Do you think anything else should be on this plan? If so, let me know. I'll take all the help I can get."

Over the past 20 years, I've enjoyed dozens of dining experiences at Jack Stack Barbecue; and I've invested several days working with the company leaders, managers, and employees over the past few months. But, nothing impacted me more than this meeting. At its end, I was able to ask the participants how they benefited from the meeting. The employees told me that they appreciated being on the same page with one another and with their managers, and acknowledged that teamwork is improving. One person observed that it's useful and appreciated knowing how the team—and the company overall—were doing. Another person said that sharing the financial information helped him feel better about his job.

And then something happened that really puts an exclamation mark on the remarkable business that is Jack Stack Barbecue.

Once the meeting concluded, I was visiting with Case and Travis when a young employee named Crystal came over to speak to Case. Crystal is studying to be a nurse for cancer patients. A few weeks earlier, she approached Case and told him that she was getting nervous about an upcoming speech she was giving on what happens to the body when a person goes through cancer treatment. Case told her to relax and present the information just like she presented it to him. He encouraged her and told her that she would do just fine. Crystal was glowing that morning when she told Case, "I got an A+ on my speech." Case smiled broadly and said, "I knew you could do it, Crystal. Good job!"

It's really possible. You *can* build an extraordinary business and live an extraordinary life. It's happening every day in businesses around the world; businesses like Jack Stack Barbecue, and businesses like yours.

Organizational Health Assessment

An Organizational Health Assessment (OHA) is a diagnostic tool to assess the capacity of an organization at six levels, from the person to the relationships, the management to the systems, the leadership to the marketplace.

Many of our clients conduct an annual OHA, similar to an annual physical, to better identify and address their issues.

How to implement an Organizational Health Assessment:

- Contact us at www.JoeCalhoon.com.
- Conduct the confidential survey.
- Use the report and recommendations to improve your organization.
- Utilize the OHA annually to measure progress and build capacity in the six areas.

Why Conduct an Organizational Health Assessment?

An Organizational Health Assessment:

- Collects confidential information from a company's employees.
- Compiles the information and defines issues that will improve organizational performance.
- Provides a measure of effectiveness than can be improved from year to year.
- Increases employee involvement in the organizational development process.
- Strengthens understanding, commitment, and morale.

See Figure A1.1 for a summary chart example.

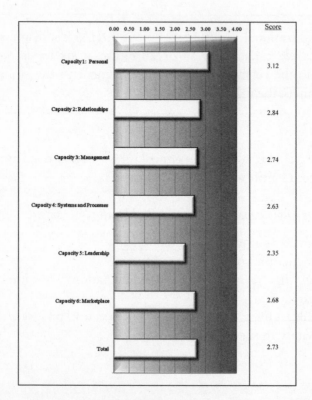

Figure A1.1   OHA Summary Chart Example

Capacity 1: Personal

The first capacity of high performance is personal—that's *you*. This capacity includes an awareness of your strengths and purpose, time management, personal development, and work/life balance. See Table A1.1.

Capacity 2: Relationships

The second capacity of high performance is relationships. This capacity includes serving one another, communication, and trust. See Table A1.2.

Capacity 3: Management

The third capacity of high performance is management. This capacity includes clear expectations, performance feedback, adequate resources, and the manager relationship. See Table A1.3.

Capacity 4: Systems and Processes

The fourth capacity of high performance is systems and processes. This capacity includes all of the systems and processes that produce quality and results. See Table A1.4.

Capacity 5: Leadership

The fifth capacity of high performance is leadership. This capacity includes planning, performance, leadership development, and organizational culture. See Table A1.5.

Capacity 6: Marketplace

The sixth capacity of high performance is the marketplace. This capacity includes reputation, marketplace intelligence, and the value you provide to customers, communities, and the world. See Table A1.6.

To complete an OHA for your organization, complete Tables A1.1–A1.6.

Table A1.1 Capacity 1: Personal

	Strongly Disagree	Disagree	Neutral	Agree	Strongly Agree
1—I have a clear understanding of my life purpose and priorities.	0	1	2	3	4
2—I understand and appreciate my unique strengths and abilities.	0	1	2	3	4
3—At work, I get to use my unique strengths and abilities every day.	0	1	2	3	4
4—At work, I spend an appropriate amount of time on what's most important.	0	1	2	3	4
5—I produce desirable results while maintaining physical, mental, and spiritual vitality.	0	1	2	3	4
6—I enjoy a healthy work/life balance.	0	1	2	3	4
Total each column	—	—	—	—	—
Add column totals			=		
Divide total score by 6 to get your Capacity 1: Personal Score			/6 = _____		

Table A1.2 Capacity 2: Relationships

	Strongly Disagree	Disagree	Neutral	Agree	Strongly Agree
7—While accomplishing my desired results, I serve the needs of others.	0	1	2	3	4
8—I consistently seek to understand others' viewpoints without interrupting.	0	1	2	3	4
9—I express my opinions and feelings with courage and consideration.	0	1	2	3	4
10—My ideas and suggestions are valued by others.	0	1	2	3	4
11—When the members of my team have an issue with someone, we confront them directly about it. We don't avoid the issues or talk to others about it.	0	1	2	3	4
12—My work relationships are characterized by unity, harmony, and trust.	0	1	2	3	4
13—I am privileged to work with a good friend.	0	1	2	3	4
14—My coworkers produce high-quality work.	0	1	2	3	4
Total each column	—	—	—	—	—
Add column totals			= ____		
Divide total score by 8 to get your Capacity 2: Relationship Score		____ /8 = ____			

Table A1.3 Capacity 3: Management

	Strongly Disagree	Disagree	Neutral	Agree	Strongly Agree
15—I have a good relationship with my manager. He or she cares about me as a person.	0	1	2	3	4
16—I understand what's expected of me at work.	0	1	2	3	4
17—I receive timely feedback on my performance. I know how well I'm doing on my job.	0	1	2	3	4
18—I always have the resources to do my work efficiently.	0	1	2	3	4
19—We consistently achieve our results on time.	0	1	2	3	4
20—My team has good relationships with other teams in the company.	0	1	2	3	4
21—I have received praise for doing good work in the last week.	0	1	2	3	4
22—We hold people accountable for their performance. We give people a chance, but people who don't produce don't stay very long.	0	1	2	3	4
Total each column	—	—	—	—	—
Add column totals			=		
Divide total score by 8 to get your Capacity 3: Management Score			/8 =		

Table A1.4 Capacity 4: Systems and Processes

	Strongly Disagree	Disagree	Neutral	Agree	Strongly Agree
23—We have effective and efficient systems for hiring, orienting, training, and developing people.	0	1	2	3	4
24—We have effective methods/systems for communication.	0	1	2	3	4
25—Work processes in my area are efficient and effective. We almost never need to do work over nor do we waste time, money, or resources.	0	1	2	3	4
26—We are good at finding, serving, and keeping customers.	0	1	2	3	4
27—We have effective systems for storing and finding information.	0	1	2	3	4
28—We have good measurement systems. It's easy to tell how we're doing in relation to our objectives.	0	1	2	3	4
29—We do a good job of planning and prevention. This minimizes crises and fire-fighting.	0	1	2	3	4
30—We are a learning organization. We are constantly getting better.	0	1	2	3	4
Total each column	—	—	—	—	—
Add column totals			=		
Divide total score by 8 to get your Capacity 4: Systems Score		/8 =			

Table A1.5 Capacity 5: Leadership

	Strongly Disagree	Disagree	Neutral	Agree	Strongly Agree
31—Our organization has a clear and compelling vision, mission, and values.	0	1	2	3	4
32—We have well-defined strategies. We know how we're going to achieve our vision.	0	1	2	3	4
33—We enjoy a high-trust culture.	0	1	2	3	4
34—As an organization, we accomplish what we set out to do.	0	1	2	3	4
35—When things change, we adjust quickly and easily.	0	1	2	3	4
36—Our organization develops effective leaders.	0	1	2	3	4
Total each column	—	—	—	—	—
Add column totals			= ___		
Divide total score by 6 to get your Capacity 5: Leadership Score	___ /6 = ___				

Table A1.6 Capacity 6: Marketplace

	Strongly Disagree	Disagree	Neutral	Agree	Strongly Agree
37—Our organization has a strong reputation.	0	1	2	3	4
38—Our organization gives back to our community and world.	0	1	2	3	4
39—We understand the current and future needs of our clientele.	0	1	2	3	4
40—We understand the trends in our industry.	0	1	2	3	4
41—Our organization's vision, mission, and values are clearly communicated and widely understood by our stakeholders.	0	1	2	3	4
42—Our organization makes a significant, positive impact.	0	1	2	3	4
Total each column	—	—	—	—	—
Add column totals			=		
Divide total score by 6 to get your Capacity 6: Marketplace Score			/6 =		

The last three questions ask:

1. What is going well in your organization?

_____
_____
_____
_____
_____
_____
_____
_____
_____
_____

2. What is not going well or what needs attention?

_____
_____
_____
_____
_____
_____
_____
_____
_____
_____

3. What else would you like to share? Is there anything else you'd like your organization to know?

_____
_____
_____
_____
_____
_____
_____
_____
_____

To further identify your issues, please complete the Organizational Health Assessment, total your scores in each area, and transfer to the OHA Summary Chart (below). Any area below 2.67 is unhealthy. A score from 2.67 to 3.00 is marginally healthy. Any score above 3.00 is healthy.

Once you've identified the capacity needing attention, refer back to Tables A1.1–A1.6 to focus on specific issues that require strategic attention.

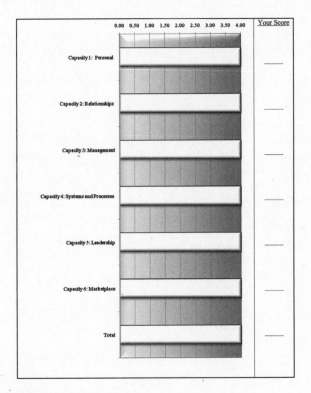

Figure A1.2   OHA Summary Chart

How to Conduct a SWOT Analysis

Most organizations develop far more strengths, weaknesses, opportunities, and threats (SWOT's) than they can address effectively, profitability, and with the available resources. They therefore boil down their long lists of SWOT's to three to five priority strategic issues they must confront if the organization is to have a healthy future.
— C. Davis Fogg, Author

> SWOT stands for internal realities (Strengths and Weaknesses) and external realities (Opportunities and Threats).

In his book *Good to Great*, Jim Collins says, "The good-to-great leaders were able to strip away so much noise and clutter and just focus on the few things that would have the greatest impact."

That's what you accomplish when you implement this time-tested approach to conducting a SWOT analysis. The process is remarkably engaging, fun, and enlightening. Your issues will comfortably rise to the surface. First, let's explore why you might want to engage your team in this activity.

Why Conduct a SWOT Analysis?

Let's imagine that you want to travel to Aspen, Colorado, to enjoy a vacation with your family. Obviously, you can't plan the trip unless you know where you are now.

Likewise in your business, after you have identified where you want to go, you'll want to clearly define where you are now. Then and only then can you effectively strategize on how you will get from here to there. The planning process always begins by defining where you want to go. It's easier to move an organization forward if you're future-focused. Focusing on the future creates a sense of hope and optimism. If you *start* the planning process by defining where you are now, people tend to get problem-focused, overwhelmed, and pessimistic.

Facilitating a SWOT analysis is a powerful way to define where you are now. A SWOT analysis will help you see the brutal realities facing your organization.

SWOT stands for Strengths, Weaknesses, Opportunities, and Threats. To get a better understanding of where you are now, you'll want to look at both your internal realities (Strengths and Weaknesses) and external realities (Opportunities and Threats). The SWOT analysis is a familiar tool to many, but many organizations could use the SWOT more efficiently and effectively.

After conducting a SWOT analysis, the major categories of work that need to be accomplished will become apparent. The result of your analysis will be a clear and concise list of issues that you will want to address in your plan. This list will help define the strategies and priorities that will help you get there. After writing your strategies and priorities in this way, circle back through your SWOT issues to ensure that action is being taken on each of the high-leverage issues.

How to Conduct an Effective SWOT Analysis

Here are three simple steps to conduct an effective SWOT analysis.

1. Assemble the right team.
2. Brainstorm the issues by using an Affinity Exercise.

3. Multivote to sort your issues in order of importance.

The first step is to assemble a group of people who understand the issues facing your organization. These issues relate to your industry, marketplace, customers, employees, owners, and other critical issues you may be facing. Ideally, this group will include your core leadership team and those responsible for producing business results. The group may include up to 12 people or so. With an effective facilitator, the group may be as large as a couple dozen people.

The second step is to conduct an Affinity Exercise. An Affinity Exercise works somewhat like a brainstorming session. Remind people of the rules of brainstorming: quantity matters more than quality; speed is good; don't stop to analyze or edit yourself. The goal is to identify a large number of issues in a short period of time.

Start with "Strengths." Give all the participants a pad of sticky notes and a felt-tip pen. Then, instruct the participants to write one Strength per sticky note. Have people write large enough so that everyone can see the writing from a few feet away. Set a time limit of two minutes. You may be surprised to learn that you don't need any more time than this. Have the participants write as many Strengths as they can in two minutes. Then call "Stop!" Have everyone go to a wall and put their notes up in random order. Just get them up there. Then have everyone work together to arrange the Strengths by categories. Talk to each other, "I've got Expertise here, anybody else see anything related to that?" In the end you'll have categories of notes together and perhaps a few orphans (Strengths that have only one sticky note each). At this point you'll want to record the categories and orphans on a flip chart. Your list may include Great People, Effective Management, Strong Customer Base, and so on. Note: If you have a large number of participants, you may want to organize the participants in teams of two to three people each to write the SWOT issues.

Now repeat the Affinity Exercise with Weaknesses, Opportunities, and Threats. At the end of this step, you will have four lists of issues on four separate flip-chart pages.

You will have one page each for Strengths, Weaknesses, Opportunities, and Threats.

There are some items that may show up on more than one list. Communication may be listed as a Strength and a Weakness.

In the end, it doesn't really matter on which list an issue shows up. All of the items from the four flip charts are issues that may require strategic attention. The most important issues become "strategic choices." They're also assigned to someone as a priority. So, whether an issue is a Strength or a Weakness it won't really matter.

Now for the third step: Multivoting. Multivoting is a way to quickly prioritize your list of most important issues using everyone's input. All the participants will receive a limited number of votes in order to identify the issues that matter most to your organization. Here's how it works:

First delete all the duplicate items; otherwise the votes will need to be combined later.

To determine how many votes everyone gets, count up the number of items remaining on all four lists. Let's say you have 35 issues (9 Strengths, 11 Weaknesses, 10 Opportunities, and 5 Threats). Divide that number by three and round up. In this case the number is 12.

So everyone gets 12 votes. They can "spend" their votes any way they want, with one restriction: No more than three votes on any one item. In other words, participants can vote once, twice, or three times on any issue, for a total of 12 votes. There's one criterion for voting. Choose only those items worthy of strategic consideration. It doesn't do you much good to identify the economy as a threat if you don't want to focus attention there.

Here's an important tip: Have people write their votes down on a piece of paper before they start recording the votes on the flip chart. That way the first few participants won't influence the other voters. Then have everybody mark their votes on the flip charts and total the votes. After everyone has voted, there is usually a clear break between a few items that get many votes and the many items that get few or no votes. The 80/20 Principle suggests that five to ten issues will get the most votes. These are the issues that need to be addressed as you write your strategies.

You will identify and prioritize your SWOT issues in less than an hour by using this approach. Everyone has participated, so you have a strong sense of buy-in when it comes time to take action.

Note: It's always acceptable for the leader to amend the multivoting process by adding an issue or two that need to be addressed. You want buy-in from the participants. You also want the best thinking of the leaders.

Sample SWOT Issues

Here are some sample issues that may be identified during a SWOT analysis.

Table A2.1

✓	Strengths	✓	Weaknesses
	Customer Service		Accountability
	Experience		Brand
	Financial Stability		Cash Flow
	Integrity		Empowerment
	Management		Inconsistent Performance
	Sales		Ineffective Marketing
	People		Inefficient Systems
	Positive Attitudes		Lack of Communication
	Reputation		Measurements
	Respect		Outdated Technology
	Location		Teamwork
	Team Work		Training

(continued)

Table A2.1 (*continued*)

✓	Opportunities	✓	Threats
	Grow Niche Markets		Bad Customers
	Outsourcing		Big Discounters
	Equipment		Competition
	Develop Partnerships		Economy
	Higher Margins		Labor Pool
	Innovation		Terrorism
	Buy a Building		Mother Nature
	Multiple Locations		Regulations
	New Business Model		Rising Costs
	New Acquisition		Tax Policy
	Self-Development		Technology Changes
	Strategic Partnerships		Vendor Failures

About the Author

In the past 25 years, Joe Calhoon has delivered more than 2,500 experiences to over 500 organizations—providing the tools and guidance needed to develop higher performing organizations. His proven process for business growth has allowed clients like Wilson Auctioneers to double revenues in one year and WGK Engineers to improve profits by 400 percent in one year. Joe's clients include a wide range of small and midsize organizations plus Fortune 100 companies, such as Host Hotels & Resorts, Helmerich & Payne, and Burns & McDonnell.

As a Certified Speaking Professional (CSP), designated through the National Speakers Association, Joe communicates the principles and practices of leadership effectiveness and organizational performance with an entertaining, educational, and inspirational style.

During the 1990s, Joe was one of the most requested and highest rated keynote speakers with the FranklinCovey Co. Joe knows the importance of synergy, communication, and effectiveness and he brings this experience to every client interaction.

Joe is the president of PriorityAdvantage™ and has co-authored *Prioritize! A System for Leading Your Business and Life on Purpose* and *On the Same Page: How to Engage Employees and Accelerate Growth.*

Joe lives with his wife Diane, their two dogs, and three cats in Kansas City, Missouri.

Additional Planning Resources

www.1Hour2Plan.com—Collaborate with your team (online) to develop your business growth plan. Involve as many people as you'd like, get their best thinking and create a plan that fits on a single sheet of paper.

Organizational Health Assessment (OHA)—Measure the capacity of your organization to grow and prosper. After your team completes the assessment, you'll receive a written report with your comparative scores and specific strategic recommendations. Coaching is also available.

Two Question (2Q) Client Satisfaction Survey—In just five minutes your customers provide you with valuable feedback. Your written report includes all of the customer data, your net promoter score, and written comments from customers.

Phone Consultation—Develop (and implement) your business growth plan with the assistance of an experienced coach.

Strategic Planning Events—Get your leadership team on the same page in less than a day. Prework includes strengths assessments, OHA, 1Hour2Plan.com, personal interviews, and consultation.

Business Growth Projects—Work with our professional team over the course of several months or several years to grow your business—guaranteed!

Keynote Speaking—Discover the keys to business growth and higher performance through compelling stories, proven processes, and actionable ideas.

1Hour2Plan: The "Live" Experience—Groups of business owners develop their own business growth plans in one to four hours.

www.JoeCalhoon.com